Snorkel Maui and Lana'i

Guide to the Underwater World of Hawai'i • Judy and Mel Malinowski

Snorkel Maui and Lanai
Guide to the Underwater World of Hawaii

Second Edition © 2001 by Judy and Mel Malinowski

Published by: Indigo Publications
920 Los Robles Avenue
Palo Alto, CA 94306 USA

SAN 298-9921
Publisher's symbol: Indigo CA

Printed in Hong Kong by C & C Offset Printing Co., Inc.

About the cover:

Camille Young painted this lovely Hinalea (yellowtail coris) in watercolor especially for our cover. A graduate of the University of Hawai'i at O'ahu, she now lives in Moraga, California.

Dave Barry is renowned for his humorous essays and books. His love of the underwater world brings a special eloquence to these passages.

Quotes from "Blub Story", Tropic Magazine, © Dave Barry 1989.

Mahalo to the kind residents of Maui and Lana'i for keeping the aloha tradition alive, Marta Jorasch, Captain Tom Allen for his contribution to the Lana'i section, and many others.

Every effort has been made to provide accurate and reliable information and advice in this book. Venturing out into the ocean has inherent, ever-changing risks which must be evaluated in each situation by the persons involved. The authors and publishers are not responsible for any inconvenience, loss or injury sustained by our readers during their travels. Travel, swim and snorkel safely. When in doubt, err on the side of caution.

ISBN 0-9646680-3-3
Library of Congress Catalog Card Number: 00-101404

First Published 1996 as Snorkel Hawaii: Maui and Lanai

Contents

Pailolo Channel

Honokohau Bay

Namalu Bay

Honolua Bay
Mokule'ia Bay

Nakalele Point

Kapalua Bay
Napili Bay
Honokeana Bay

30

KAHAKULOA

Ho'okipa Park

Honokowai Park

Kapalua
West Maui
Airport

WEST MAUI MOUNTAINS

Kahului
Airport

Kanaha
Beach

Kahekili Beach

KA'ANAPALI

340

WAIHE'E

36

Ka'anapali Beach

WAILUKU

Hanakao'o Beach

30

WEST
MAUI

32

37

Lahaina Harbor

LAHAINA

Pu'u Kuka'i
5,788'

'Iao Needle
2,250'

KAHULUI

Haleakala
Hwy.

Puamana Beach

380

Launiupoko Wayside

'Auau Channel

Olowalu Beach

Honoapi'ilani Hwy.

30

350

Kealia Pond

Ukumehame Beach
Papalaua Wayside

Ma'alaea
Bay

KIHEI

Papawai Point

31

Kalama Beach

Ma'alaea Harbor

Kama'ole I, II, & III

SOUTH
MAUI

Keawakapu Beach

Mokapu Beach
Ulua Beach
Wailea Beach
Polo Beach

WAILEA

37

Maluaka Beach

MAKENA

Pu'u 'ola'i Beach
Oneloa Beach

Pu'u 'Ola'i
360'

Molokini Island

'Ahihi Bay

'Ahihi-Kina'u Reserve

'Alalakeiki Channel

La Perouse Bay

Kanaio
Coast

4

Maui

(Also see Maui Snorkeling Site Index Map on page 38)

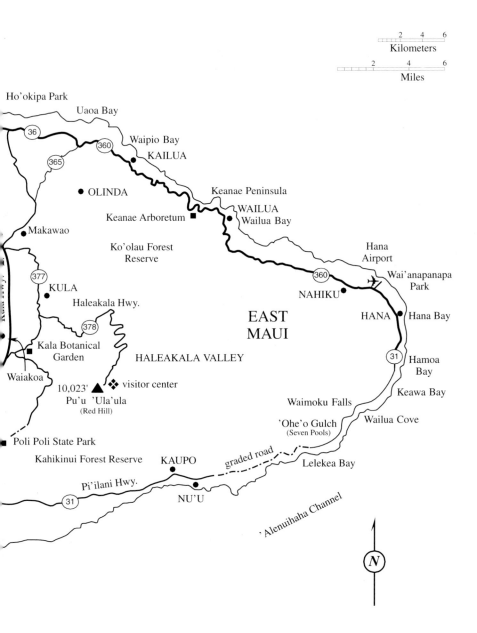

2   4   6
Kilometers

2   4   6
Miles

Ho'okipa Park

Uaoa Bay

36

360   Waipio Bay

365   KAILUA

OLINDA   Keanae Peninsula

Keanae Arboretum   WAILUA
                          Wailua Bay

Makawao

Ko'olau Forest
Reserve   Hana
                                     Airport

377   Wai'anapanapa
                                     360   Park
KULA
                          NAHIKU
Haleakala Hwy.   HANA   Hana Bay
                     EAST
378   MAUI
Kala Botanical   31   Hamoa
Garden   HALEAKALA VALLEY   Bay

Waiakoa   Keawa Bay

10,023' ▲ ❖ visitor center   Waimoku Falls   Wailua Cove
Pu'u 'Ula'ula
(Red Hill)   'Ohe'o Gulch
                             (Seven Pools)

Poli Poli State Park

Kahikinui Forest Reserve   KAUPO   graded road   Lelekea Bay

Pi'ilani Hwy.
31   NU'U

'Alenuihaha Channel

N

To Sophie, Ethan and Olivia Jorasch.
May they come to know and love the
underwater world as we have.

Why Snorkel Maui?

Maui offers more snorkeling sites within easy reach than any other Hawai'ian island. There is something here for every snorkeler and ample variety to keep a whole family happy.

Laze around on endless golden beaches and cool yourself with colorful snorkeling swims. Follow this up with good food, shopping and socializing if you're so inclined. It's all close at hand on Maui.

There are many sites with easy entry from calm, sheltered bays and broad, golden sandy beaches. Maui has extensive reefs with plenty of colorful and exciting creatures. Popular Molokini Island, with its crystal-clear waters, or the unique island of Lana'i lie just a brief excursion away, and offer a change of pace if you're in the mood.

The choices are ample: beautiful, sweeping expanses of soft coral sand and diverse snorkeling sites; action-packed total destination resorts with all amenities; secluded little-known beach retreats just around the bend; or nearby, less touristed neighbor island hideaways. Choices like this have made Maui a legendary destination.

Snorkel Maui and Lana'i makes it easy

An active vacation is memorable for adventure as well as relaxation. Hassles and missteps finding out where to go can raise your blood pressure and waste your time. We've done extensive research that will help you quickly locate appropriate sites that fit your interests and abilities, saving your valuable vacation hours.

Snorkeling sites in Hawai'i are sometimes tricky because of changeable waves and currents, so it's best to get good advice before heading out. Everyone has had their share of unpleasant experiences due to vague directions as well as outdated or inaccurate information. We have created the Snorkel Hawai'i series as that savvy snorkeling buddy everyone needs. We've included many personal stories; see About the Authors on page 192 if you want to know a little more about us.

We have snorkeled all the major sites listed many times, and many that are not well known. The challenge lies in finding them quickly, as well as how to enter and exit, and where to snorkel, so you'll have a safe and rewarding experience. Our detailed maps and instructions will ease the uncertainty, saving you time and effort.

Try to visit Maui and Lana'i at least once in your life and by all means don't miss the underwater world. Aloha!

–Judy and Mel Malinowski

- easy
- relaxing
- fun
- floating on the surface of the sea
- breathing without effort through a tube
- peering into the water world through a mask
- open to any age, size, shape or ability

Who was the first snorkeler? As the fossil records include few petrified snorkels, we are free to speculate.

Among larger creatures, elephants are the pioneers and current champions, as they have known how to snorkel for countless generations. Once in a blue moon, you may see a elephant herd heading out to do lunch on an island off the coast of Tanzania, paddling along with their trunks held high. No one knows whether the hefty pachyderms enjoy the fish-watching, but you can bet a big liquid chuckle reverberates through the ranks of reef fish in the vicinity as the parade goes by.

As evolution continued, perhaps a clever member of the promising homo sapiens species saved his furry brow by hiding underwater from pursuers, breathing through a hollow reed. Masks came much later, so the fish probably looked a little fuzzy. Surviving to propagate his brainy kind, he founded a dynasty of snorkelers. Perhaps he actually liked the peaceful atmosphere down there, and a new sport was born.

Some of our readers may grumble that snorkeling is not a real sport: no rules, no score, no competition, scarcely aerobic, with hardly any equipment or clothing. We say to them: lighten up, you're on vacation!! Go for a long run later.

Incorrigible competitors can create their own competition by counting how many species they've seen or trying to spot the biggest or the most seen in one day. Everybody else can relax and just have fun being a part of nature's colorful, salty, wet, ancient home.

Basics

To snorkel you need only two things:

Snorkel	Saves lifting your head once a minute, wasting energy and disturbing the fish.
Mask	While you can see (poorly) without one, it keeps the water out of your eyes and lets you see clearly.

Rent them inexpensively at many local shops or buy them if you prefer. It's all the back-to-basics folks need to snorkel in calm warm water, where there aren't any currents or hazards.

Savvy snorkelers often add a few items to the list, based on years of experience, such as:

Swimsuit	Required by law in many localities. Added benefit: can save you from an occasional all-body sunburn.
Fins	Good if you want to swim with ease and speed like a fish. Saves energy. A must in Hawai'i, due to occasional strong currents. They protect your tender feet too.
T-shirt	Simple way to avoid or minimize sunburn on your back. Available everywhere in Lahaina and Kihei.
Sunscreen	To slather on the tender exposed backside skin of your legs, neck, and the backs of your arms. Not optional in Hawai'i for light-skinned snorkelers.
Lycra Skin	A great all body coverup for warm weather. Provides much better protection than a T-shirt, and saves gallons of sunscreen.
Wetsuit	For some, the Hawai'ian waters seem a bit chilly – not exactly pool-warm. Wetsuits range from simple T-shirt-like tops to full suits. Worth considering. Fringe benefit: free sun protection!

You're almost ready to get wet. But wait! You want to know even more technical detail? Every sport has an equipment list – it's what keeps sporting goods stores in business and your garage shelves full.

Gear Selection

Good snorkeling gear enables you to pay attention to the fish instead of uncomfortable distractions. Poor equipment will make you suffer in little ways, from pressure headaches caused by a too-tight mask, to blisters on your feet from ill-fitting fins. Consider your alternatives carefully before buying and you'll have more fun later.

Snorkel

Snorkels can be quite cheap. Be prepared to pony up $15 or more if you want them to last awhile and be comfortable. You'll appreciate a comfortable mouthpiece if you plan to snorkel for long. Watch out for hard edges – a good mouthpiece is smooth and chewy-soft.

Several new high tech models have been designed to minimize water coming down the tube from chop or an occasional swell overtopping you. We looked at these with mild skepticism until a choppy snorkeling trip had us coughing and clearing our snorkels every third breath. With our new snorkels, that water is diverted out before it makes it to the mouthpiece.

We tested a new snorkel by pouring buckets of water down the tube. The snorkeler didn't even notice! Our verdict is: the new technology works as advertised. Avoid the old "float ball at the top" versions.

We use the US Divers Impulse snorkel (about $35), but others may be equally effective. A friend recommends a Dacor model with corrugated, flexible neck. A bottom purge valve makes blowing out water smooth and easy, on those occasional cases when it is required. These nifty snorkels are well worth the higher price if you snorkel in choppy water or like to surface dive.

Snorkel Holder

This little guy holds your snorkel to your mask strap, so you don't keep dipping it in the sea. The standard is a simple figure 8 double loop that pulls over the snorkel tube, wraps around your mask strap, and then back over the tube. A hefty rubber band will work passably in a pinch.

The higher end snorkels often have a slot that allows the snorkel to be adjusted easily. It slides rather than having to be tugged. The standard Scuba snorkel position is on your left side. You might as well get used to it there since you may dive eventually.

Mask

Nothing can color your snorkeling experience more than an ill-fitting mask. Unless, of course, you get that all-body sunburn mentioned earlier. Don't settle for painful or leaky masks! If it hurts, it's not your problem – it's the mask that's wrong for you. In this case "pain, no gain" applies.

Simple variety store masks can cost as little as $10. Top-quality masks from a dive shop run upwards of $60. Consider starting out with a rental mask, paying a bit extra for the better quality models. As you gain more experience, you'll be in a better position to evaluate a mask before you lock yourself into one style.

You need a good fit to your particular facial geometry. Shops often tell you to place the mask on your face (without the strap) and breathe in. If the mask will stay in place, then they say you have found a good fit. However, nearly all masks will stay on my face under this test, yet some leak later!

Look for soft edges and a mask that conforms to your face even before drawing in your breath. There's a great deal of variance in where a mask rests on your face and how soft it feels, so compare very carefully. Look for soft and comfortable, unless you especially like having pressure headaches and don't mind looking like a very large octopus glommed on to your face.

Lack of 20-20 vision needn't cut into your viewing pleasure, but it does require a little more effort during equipment selection. Those who wear contact lenses can use them within their masks, taking on the risk that they'll swish out and float softly and invisibly down to the sea bed, perhaps to be found by a fossil hunter in the distant future, but certainly not by you. Use the disposable kind. Unless you use contacts, search for a correctable mask. Vision-correcting lens are available for many masks in 1/2 diopter increments.

parrotfish

If the mask you prefer doesn't offer standard correcting lenses, custom prescription lenses can be fitted to almost any mask. This costs more and takes longer. Even bifocals are available. We happen to prefer the comfortable prescription masks made by SeaVision which can be ordered with any custom correction. The cost is much like normal prescription lenses.

Mustaches create a mask leakage problem. As I like the look of a mustache, I have coped with this my entire adult life. Some advise the use petroleum jelly to make a more effective seal. That doesn't appeal to me since I go in and out of the water several times a day. It does help to choose a mask that rests high over the mouth and perhaps trim the top 1/8 inch or so off the center mustache, if it sticks up. Hair breaks the seal and allows water to seep into the mask slowly, so you'll still have to clear the mask occasionally.

Someone who has struggled with a leaky mask may prefer having a purge valve. There are some clever higher-end purge valve masks. The challenge is how to fit in a purge valve without making it harder to pinch your nose to equalize your ears when surface or scuba diving.

The conventional wisdom in Scuba is that purge valves are an unnecessary weak point. Nevertheless, there are experienced divers who use them. This isn't an issue snorkelers need worry about. If you find a purge valve mask that fits well, use it.

Mask Strap

The strap that comes with the mask is generally fine, but if you have your own mask and want it to slide on more easily, there's a comfortable strap available with adjustment by velcro. The back is made of wetsuit material – stretchy and soft. Cost is about $12 in dive shops. Since we get in and out so often, we happen to prefer this one to the regular strap, but it's a convenience for the frequent snorkeler rather than a necessity.

convict tang

Low Volume Masks

When you begin looking at masks, the variety can be bewildering. How can you figure out which design is best for you?

Inexpensive masks tend to have one large flat front glass. They're OK if the skirt of the mask fits you, although they're often a bit stiff and uncomfortable. They also tend to be far out from your face with a big air space. As you go up in price, the lenses tend to get smaller and closer to your eyes, as preferred by divers. There is a good Scuba reason for this. These are called "low volume" masks. They contain less airspace and so require less effort to clear when water gets in. They also press less against your face when you go deeper and the pressure rises (if you forget to blow higher pressure air in through your nose) and hence are more comfortable when diving.

For a snorkeler this is of little importance, but it still should be considered as you select your mask. Many snorkelers go on to do some surface diving, as well as Snuba or Scuba diving. When you dive down even 10', the water pressure is considerable. At 32', the air in your lungs and mask is compressed to half its volume, and unless you remember to blow some air into your mask through your nose, the pressure on your face can be most uncomfortable!

If your mask is flooded, which does happen occasionally, it is easier to clear out the water from a low volume mask. So, while it's not the most important factor, if everything else is equal, low volume is better.

Fins

The simplest fins are basic (usually black) enclosed foot fins. These are one-piece molded rubber and slip right on to your bare feet. For warm water, basic snorkeling, these inexpensive fins are fine. We own several kinds of fins and still often choose the one-piece foot fins for lightness and compact packing. They seem to last forever and are inexpensive ($15–$25).

Why should anyone look further? Because it is possible to get better comfort and more thrust. Specialized fins are now made for higher performance. We tested three sets of fins, doing timed swims over a measured course. The basic fins discussed above went first. A set of fairly expensive, but rather soft, flexible strap-on fins cut the swim time by 20%, while ultra long, stiff-bladed foot-mount Cressi fins cut it by 40%! These long surface diving fins are, however, a little long and awkward to use for most surface snorkeling.

Opinions vary about the merits of flexible fin blades versus stiff blades. We've tested both for snorkeling, and we prefer light, thin, stiff blades, hands down. We also prefer fins that don't float, which isn't an issue with Scuba divers, but can reduce a snorkeler's efficiency if it holds the fins too high in the water.

You're better off with a medium blade foot fin for most snorkeling. Large diving fins are awkward for snorkeling, and require more leg strength than most non-athletes possess. The big diving fins do come in numerous shapes and colors, which some people are convinced will make them faster or perhaps more attractive. Speed is not the main aim of snorkeling, but has its uses. Faster fins do enable you to cover more territory and they also serve as excellent insurance in case you wander into a strong current. Unless it's absolutely certain that no current can carry you away, ALWAYS WEAR FINS!

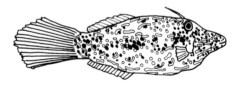

scrawled filefish

As you look at more advanced fins, they split into two attachment methods with pros and cons to each type. We own both and pick the best for a particular situation.

ENCLOSED FOOT	Your bare foot slides into a stretchy, integral molded rubber shoe.
Advantages	The lightest, most streamlined and fish-like fit. It probably is the most efficient at transmitting your muscle power to the blade. We prefer this type when booties are not required for warmth or safety.
Disadvantages	The fins must be closely fitted to your particular foot size. Some models may cause blisters. If you have to hike in to the entry site, you need separate shoes. This may preclude entering at one spot, and exiting elsewhere. If you hike over rough ground (a'a lava, for example) to get to your entry point, or the entry is over sharp coral or other hazards, these may not be the best choice.
STRAP-ON	Made for use with booties.
Advantages	Makes rough surface entry easy. Just hike to the entry point, head on into the water holding your fins in hand, lay back and pull on your fins. Exiting is just as easy. The bootie cushions your foot, making blisters unlikely. Widely used for Scuba.
Disadvantages	Less streamlined. The bootie makes your feet float up, so you may have trouble keeping your fins from breaking the surface.

No matter how good the fins, snorkeling for long hours may cause blisters – especially on the heel. No need to worry if you carry 3M Nexcare waterproof bandages. These little essentials will do the job and stay in place well when wet. Buy them at a major pharmacy before your trip – they can be hard to find in the islands.

Reef Shoes or Booties

Walking with bare feet on a'a (sharp lava) or coral can shred your feet in a quick minute. There are fine reef shoes available that are happy in or out of the water. These are primarily for getting there, or wading around, as they don't really work that well with strap-on fins. For the sake of the reef, don't actually walk on a reef with reef shoes, since each step kills hundreds of the little animals that make up the living reef.

Zip-on booties are widely used by divers and allow use of strap-on fins. They do float your feet – a disadvantage for snorkelers.

Keeping Time

One easy-to-forget item: a water-resistant watch. This needn't be expensive and is very useful for pacing yourself and keeping track of your sun exposure time.

"Water resistant" alone usually means that a little rain won't wreck the watch, but immersion in water may. When a designation like "to 10 meters" is added, it denotes added water-resistance; but the dynamic pressures from swimming increase the pressure, so choose 50 meters or greater rating to be safe even when snorkeling. Don't take a 50 meter watch Scuba diving, though – that requires 100-200 meter models.

Hawai'ian time is two hours earlier than Pacific Standard Time or three hours earlier than Pacific Daylight Time. Hawai'i doesn't observe Daylight Savings Time.

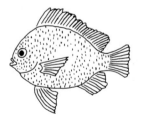

Hawai'ian damselfish

Body Suit

There are a variety of all-body suits that protect you from sun exposure and light abrasion, but provide no warmth. They are made from various synthetic fabrics – lycra and nylon being common. They cost much less than wetsuits and are light and easy to pack. We usually bring ours along as a sun protection alternative in warmer conditions. If you don't want to look like a F.O.B. (Fresh Off the Boat) tourist, with a shocking pink outline of your swimsuit, plan ahead about sun protection. You'll sleep better if you do too. And the fish will not miss all that sunscreen fouling their water.

Wetsuit

In Maui average water temperature on the surface varies from a low of about 77° F in March to a high of about 80° F in September. If you happen to be slender, no longer young or from a moderate climate, this can seem cold. Sheltered bays and tidepools can be a bit warmer while deeper water can be surprisingly cold. Fresh water runoff from coastal springs can also make water cooler than you might expect. We've snorkeled in March when we swore it was not above 65° F off Kaua'i.

Regardless of the exact temperature, the water is cooler than your body. With normal exertion, your body still cools bit by bit. After awhile, perhaps 30-45 minutes, you start feeling a little chilly. Later you begin shivering and eventually hypothermia begins.

We like to snorkel for two or more hours sometimes. A thin wetsuit protects us from the sun while keeping us warm and comfortable. Off the rack suits are a bargain and fit most folks. Look for a snug fit at neck, wrists and ankles – if your suit is loose there, water will flow in and out, making you cold. If you have big feet and small ankles, get zippers on the legs if possible or you'll really have to struggle to remove the suit when it's wet.

Wetsuit wearers get added range and buoyancy. Wetsuit wearers hardly need a life jacket! Wearing a wetsuit, you can stay in the water without hypothermia for many hours – even in the winter. This could be comforting in the unlikely event that some strong current sweeps you off towards Fiji. There are few situations from which you can't rescue yourself if you're wearing a wetsuit and fins.

We recently discovered a new technology we like a lot: Henderson Gold Core wetsuits, made in Millville, New Jersey. The inside of this suit is coated with a gold-colored nylon that slides on like a breeze wet or dry, and the inner surface dries very quickly. The three millimeter-thick version is light, warm enough for Hawai'i snorkeling and has extra stretch so it's comfortable and easy to get on and off.

Even Gold Core slides poorly on skin with dried on sticky saltwater (as when you're getting in and out frequently on a multi-stop boat trip), though better than regular wetsuits. We found, however, that if you get wet first (in a beach shower, boat shower, or jumping in), Gold Core slides on like teflon.

Dave Barry once described putting on a wetsuit as like wrestling with an octopus. Not this one! No more hanging onto the shower while your buddy tries to pull the wetsuit off your ankles with a winch. If you can afford the extra cost, the suit is superb. We had ours custom-made with longer arms and legs, and no rubberized kneepads. We like our wetsuits sleek and flexible.

Swim Cap

If you have trouble with long hair tangling in your mask straps while snorkeling, get a lycra Speedo swim cap. It may look silly, but it works, and also protects your scalp from too many rays.

Snorkeling Vest

It is possible to buy inflatable vests made for snorkeling. Some guidebooks and stores promote them as virtually essential. We've taken excursions that require all snorkelers to wear one. Other excursions encourage the use of floatation "noodles" or kick boards – whatever it takes to make you comfortable.

Vests are hardly necessary in salt water for most people, but can be useful if you can't swim a lick or won't be willing to try this sport without it. There is a possible safety edge for kids or older folks. If you do get a vest, you can give it to another beginner after you get used to snorkeling. You will discover that it takes little effort to float flat in the water while breathing through a snorkel.

If you want extra flotation, consider using a light wetsuit instead. It simultaneously gives you buoyancy, sun and critter protection, and warmth.

Surface Diving Gear

For surface diving, bigger fins help your range. Those surreal-looking Cressi fins that seem about three feet long will take you down so fast you'll be amazed. You'll also be amazed how few suitcases are wide enough to accommodate them.

A long-fin alternative is to use a soft weight belt with from 2 to 4 pounds (more if you wear a wetsuit) – just enough to help you get under the surface without using up all your energy. As you descend, you become neutrally buoyant at about 15-20 feet so you don't have to fight popping up. Of course, the sword cuts two ways, since you must swim up under your own power in time to breathe.

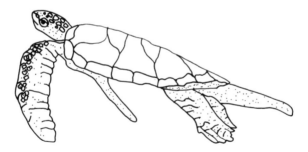

green sea turtle

Into the Water

Getting Started

Now that you've assembled a nice collection of snorkel gear, you're ready to go! On a sunny tropical morning you're down at the water's edge. Little one-foot waves slap the sand lightly, while a soft warm breeze takes the edge off the intensity of the climbing sun. It's a great day to be alive and out in the water.

Going snorkeling, it's better to have no suntan lotion on your face or hands. You sure don't want it washing into your eyes to make them burn and water. Wear a nice big hat instead. You applied lotion to your back before you left, so it had time to become effective. Then you washed off your hands and rinsed them well so the lotion couldn't contaminate your mask later.

Or you could do like we do, and skip all the lotion. Being outside as much as we are, and in and out of the water, we prefer to carefully cover up instead – we find too much lotion hard on our skin. Big broad hats like your boat captain wears help. Comfortable cotton cover-ups look good and are cool. Lycra body suits or wetsuits in the water let you stay in for as long as you wish. Do watch out for reflected light on long boat trips, which can sneak in and sizzle your tender face.

Checking Conditions

Take it nice and slow. Sit down and watch the waves for awhile. Check the slope of the beach. Consider whether there might be currents. Look for wave patterns, how big the biggest waves are and how far they wash up on the beach. When you see the pattern, you're ready to go. Set your gear down back well beyond the furthest watermarks on the sand. You don't want that seventh wave to sweep your gear away! Watch as long as it takes to be sure conditions aren't changing for the worse.

Gearing Up

Now defog the mask so that water vapor from your nose, or water leakage, won't bead up on your mask lens and spoil your view. There are two ways to defog.

The classic solution is: SPIT. Spit on the inside of your dry mask lens, and rub it all around with your sunscreen-free finger. Step into the water, just out beyond the stirred up sand, and dip up a mask full of clear saltwater. Thoroughly rub and rinse off that spit, and dump the mask. Now you have prepared a mask that should be fog-resistant for an average snorkel.

If you spit and polish, and still have fogging problems, there are several possible causes. Your mask may be gooped up with cosmetics, dried on saltwater residue or whatever other goo may be out there. A good cleaning with toothpaste may be in order (see Caring for Your Gear, page 192).

It's possible that you didn't actually wet all the surface with spit; perhaps because there were drops of water left on the lens. In that case, or if you just feel funny about spitting in your mask, you can use no-fog solution. No-fog solution for masks actually does work even better than spit. It comes in small, handy, inexpensive bottles that seem to last forever because you use only a few drops at a time. If you prefer to make your own, half baby shampoo and half water works fine.

Our favorite trick is to pre-apply no-fog solution to the dry masks an hour or more ahead and let it dry. When you get to the water, just rinse out the mask thoroughly. This seems to last a long time.

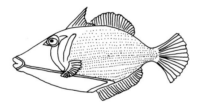

lei triggerfish

Getting Comfortable

After you rinse your mask, try its fit. Adjust the mask strap and snorkel until they're comfortable. Hold the snorkel in your mouth without tightening your jaws. It can be quite loose without falling out. Putting your mask on long before you enter the water can cause it to fog from your exertions

Getting Wet

Now retrieve your fins and walk back in the water, watching the waves carefully. NEVER turn your back on the ocean for long, lest a rogue wave sneak up on you and whack you good. The key is to stay alert and awake – especially on entry and exit.

Snorkeling is Easier than Swimming

Some folks never learn to snorkel because they're not confident as swimmers. This is an unnecessary loss because snorkeling is actually easier than swimming. We have maintained this to friends for years, and noted their doubtful looks. Recently, we came across a program in California that actually uses snorkeling as a tool to help teach swimming!

The Transpersonal Swimming Institute in California specializes in the teaching of adults who are afraid of the water. Local heated pools are used all year. But the warm, salty and buoyant ocean is the best pool of all.

Melon Dash, Director of TSI, takes groups of her students to Hawai'i where they begin by floating comfortably in the warm, salty water. At their own pace, they gradually learn to snorkel and feel comfortable in the water. For people further from California, a video called The Miracle Swimmer is available by mail.

"We have found that people cannot learn what to do with their arms and legs while they are afraid that they might not live."

With a steady air supply and not having to worry about breathing in water accidentally, they can relax and learn the arm and leg movements at ease. Happily, they soon discover there's nothing complicated about it!

In calm conditions and warm water, there need be no age limits and few physical limits for snorkeling.

Transpersonal Swimming Institute   (800) 723-7946
P.O. Box 6543   (510) 526-6000
Albany, CA 94706-0543   fax (510) 526-6091

Transwim@aol.com   www.conquerfear.com

If the bottom is sandy smooth, wade on out until you're about waist deep. Pull your mask on, making sure you remove any stray hair from under the skirt. Position the snorkel in your mouth and start breathing. You can practice this in a pool or hot tub.

Duck down in the water so you're floating and pull on your fins just like sneakers. Be sure no sand is trapped in the fins. Make a smooth turn to your stomach, pause to float and relax until you're comfortable, and you're off! Flip those fins and you have begun your re-entry into the sea.

As you float, practice steady breathing through the snorkel. Breathe slowly and deeply. People sometimes tense up at first and take short breaths. When this happens, you're only getting stale air from the snorkel rather than lots of fresh air from outside. If you ever feel tired or out of breath, don't take off your mask. Just stop as long as necessary, float, breathe easy and relax.

After you've become quite comfortable breathing this way, check how your mask is doing. Make sure it isn't leaking. Adjust the strap if needed. And keep adjusting until it's just right. Slide your snorkel strap to a comfortable position, with the tube pointing about straight up as you float looking down at about a 30° angle.

Swimming while snorkeling is easy once you've relaxed. No arms are required. What works best is to hold your arms straight back along your sides, keep your legs fairly straight and kick those fins slowly without bending your knees much. Any swimming technique will work, of course, but some are more tiring. Practice using the least amount of energy. Once you learn how to snorkel the easy way, you can use all the power you like touring large areas as if you were a migrating whale. But if you're breaking the surface with your fins, going "splash, plunk, splash", you're wasting energy. Be cool and smooth and quiet like a fish.

Clearing Your Mask

Eventually you will need to practice clearing your mask. The Scuba method: take a deep breath, then tip your head up, but with the mask still under the surface. Press your palm to the top of the mask against your forehead, or hold your fingers on the top of the mask and exhale through your nose. This forces water out the bottom of the mask.

Taking it Easy

Relax and try not to push yourself too hard. Experienced snorkelers may urge you on faster than you're comfortable because they've forgotten how it feels to get started. As your experience builds, you'll find it easy too. It's like learning to drive a car. Remember how even a parking lot seemed like a challenge? It helps to practice your beginning snorkeling in a calm easy place – with a patient teacher. With a little persistence, you'll soon overcome your fears and be ready. Don't feel like you should rush. Play around and have fun!

Knowing Your Limits

Have you heard the old saloon saying: "Don't let your mouth write checks that your body can't cover"?

Let's paraphrase this as "Don't let your ego take you places your body can't get you back from." Consider carefully how well-conditioned your legs are, so you'll have enough reserve to be able to make it back home, and then some in case of an emergency.

Snorkeling Alone

In your enthusiasm for the reef, you may wind up in this situation: your significant other prefers watching sports on ESPN to snorkeling one afternoon, and you're sorely tempted to just head out there alone. Don't do it. Snorkeling, done in buddy teams, is a pretty safe recreation, especially if conditions are favorable. Just as in Scuba diving, having a buddy along reduces the risk of a small problem becoming a big problem or even a fatal problem. We won't spell out all the bad things that could happen; we trust your imagination.

Pacing

When you're having a good time, it's easy to forget and over-extend yourself. That next rocky point beckons, and then a pretty spot beyond that. Pretty soon, you're many miles from home and getting tired. Getting cold and overly tired can contribute to poor judgement in critical situations, making you more vulnerable to injury. Why risk turning your great snorkeling experience into a disaster? Learn your limits, and how to pace yourself.

Our favorite technique: If we plan on a 1 hour snorkel, we watch the time and start heading back when we've been in the water 30 minutes. If the currents could run against us on the way back, we allow extra time/energy. We like to start by swimming against the current, making the trip home easy and quick.

Caring for Your Gear

You just had a great snorkeling experience – now you can thank the gear that helped make it possible, by taking good care of it.

Rinse and Dry

If there are beach showers, head right up and rinse off. Salt residue is sticky and corrosive. Rinse salt and sand off your wetsuit, fins, mask and snorkel before the saltwater dries. If you can, dry your gear in the shade. It's amazing how much damage sun can do to the more delicate equipment – especially the mask. When the sun odometer hits 100,000 miles, you can kiss those silicon parts goodbye.

Safety Inspections

Keep an eye on vulnerable parts after a few years (strap, snorkel-holder, buckles). Parts are usually easy to find in Hawai'i, but not in the middle of a snorkeling trip unless you're on a well-equipped boat.

If you use any equipment with purge valves, keep an eye on the delicate little flap valves, and replace them when they deteriorate. Masks and snorkels are useless when the valves give way. Remember that many snorkels now have a purge valve at the bottom.

Clean Your Mask

A mask needs a thorough cleaning between trips as well. Unless your mask instructions advise otherwise, use a regular, non-gel toothpaste to clean the lens inside and out, polishing off accumulated goo. Wash the toothpaste off with warm water, using your finger to clean it well.

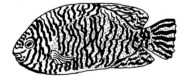

Potter's angelfish

Hazards

Life just isn't safe. Snorkeling has a few hazards that you should know and avoid if possible. You already know the dangers of car and air travel, yet you mustered your courage and decided that a trip to Hawai'i was worth the risks. And you took reasonable precautions like buckling your seat belt. Well, if you use your noggin, you're probably safer in the water than while driving to get to the water.

Some people are hesitant to snorkel because they imagine meeting a scary creature in the water. But wouldn't you rather be able to see what's down there when you're swimming? We much prefer to see whatever you might step on, run into or encounter. The realities are seldom scary.

We don't think it makes sense to overemphasize certain lurid dangers (sharks!) and pay no attention to the more likely hazard of sunburn which causes more aggravation to tourists.

Sunburn

This is the worst medical problem you're likely to face – especially if you have the wrong ancestors. Use extra water-resistant sunblock in the water and always wear some kind of cover-up during the day. Some people need to avoid the sun entirely from 10:00 a.m. to 3:00 p.m., so that's a good excuse to go early and avoid the crowds. The top (or open) deck of a boat is a serious hazard to the easily-burned because bounced rays from the water will double your exposure. The best protection is covering up. Evidence mounts that sunscreen still allows skin damage even though it stops burning. Thanks to global warming, we all get more sun in a given hour than we did ten years ago.

When snorkeling, omit sunscreen on your face or hands, because you'll be sorry later if you get the stuff in your eyes. It can really sting and make it difficult to see well enough to navigate back to shore. To avoid using gallons of sunblock, some snorkelers wear lycra body suits. Others simply wear some old clothing.

Take an old sun hat to leave on the beach with your gear bag, especially if you have to hike midday across a reflective white beach. Take old sunglasses that are not theft-worthy. If you must leave prescription glasses on the beach, use your old ones. Maui is a great place to find amazingly cheap sunglasses and flip-flops. For long hours in the sun, look into the better sunglasses that carefully filter all the most damaging rays.

Understanding Waves

Waves are travelling ripples in the water, mostly generated by wind blowing over large expanses of water. Having energy, the waves keep going until something stops them. They may travel many thousands of miles before dissipating that energy. Here is the wellspring of the breaking surf. That beautiful surf can also be the biggest danger facing snorkelers.

Take time to sit on a high point and watch the waves approaching the coast, and you will see patterns emerge. Usually there is an underlying groundswell from one direction, waves that may have originated in distant storms. This is the main source of the rhythmical breaking waves, rising and falling in size in noticeable patterns. Often, there will be a series of small waves, followed by one or more larger waves, and the cycle repeats. Pay attention to the patterns and it will be less likely that you'll get caught by surprise.

Local winds add their own extra energy in their own directions. In Hawai'i, snorkeling is usually easiest in the mornings, before the daily winds create larger waves in the afternoon. Most excursions head out early to make sure they have smooth sailing and calm snorkeling.

Occasionally a set of larger waves or a single large rogue wave comes in with little or no warning. A spot that was protected by an offshore reef suddenly has breaking waves.

Our single worst moment in many years of snorkeling and diving was at Brenneke's Beach in Kaua'i after Hurricane Iniki had scattered boulders throughout the beach. We had no problem snorkeling around the boulders in a light swell, protected by reef further out. Suddenly much larger waves crossed the reef and began breaking over us, sweeping everyone back and forth against the boulders. Since then we have been extra careful to avoid potentially hazardous situations. We always take time to study the waves before entering and ponder what would happen if they suddenly grew much larger, and what our strategy would be. Sometimes we just head for a calmer beach.

Rip Currents

Hawai'i does not have large barrier reefs to intercept incoming waves. Few of Maui's beaches are well-protected from powerful ocean currents – especially in the winter or during storms.

Waves breaking against a shore push volumes of water up close to the shore. As this piles up, it has to flow back to the ocean, and often flows sideways along the shore until it reaches a convenient, often deeper-bottomed, exit point. There, a fast, narrow river of water flows out at high speed. Rip currents, which can carry swimmers out quickly, are of limited duration by their very nature and usually stop no more than 100 yards out.

Sometimes it's possible to swim sideways, but often it's better to simply ride it out. Don't panic. Although the current might be very strong, it won't take you far or drown you, unless you exhaust yourself by swimming against it. It's very easy to float in salt water until help arrives – assuming you're at a beach where someone can see you. Don't try to swim in through waves where there's any chance of being mashed on lava rocks or coral. Don't swim against the current to the point of exhaustion. When in doubt, float and conserve energy.

Even at the most protected beaches (like Kapalua Bay), all the water coming in must get out, so when swells are up, there's a current somewhere. Big waves beyond the breakwater may seem harmless, but the more water comes in, the more must get out. This is a good reason to ALWAYS wear fins.

Rip currents should not be confused with offshore currents, such as the infamous "Tahiti Express". There are some major flows of water offshore that can be faster than you can swim. Do be alert and careful if you swim out beyond rocky points. Or send us a postcard from Tahiti.

Hypothermia

Open ocean water is always cooler than your body, and it cools you off more rapidly than the air. With normal exertion, your body still cools bit by bit. After awhile (perhaps 30-45 minutes) most of us start feeling chilly. Later, shivering begins. When your temperature drops even further, hypothermia sets in. When your body temperature has dropped enough, your abilities to move and even think become impaired.

We used to think hypothermia was just an interesting concept, until it happened to us after a long snorkel in some unusually cold water. We were shivering, but having a great time, and snorkeled on and on. Fortunately, we noticed the decrease in our co-ordination and headed in while we could. You'd have laughed to see us stumbling out of the waves. We went straight for the nearest jacuzzi. As we warmed up, our limbs tingled like fizzy water was going through our veins.

One of the first symptoms of hypothermia is poor judgement. Buddies can watch out for each other better than you can watch out for yourself alone – one example of the benefits of having a partner. Check up on each other often in cold conditions.

As soon as you are aware that you're cold, it's time to plan your way back. When shivering starts, you should get out of the water. Be particularly careful in situations requiring all your judgement and skill to be safe, especially when diving, night snorkeling, dealing with waves, or when anticipating a difficult exit from the water.

In Maui it's usually easy to warm up rapidly since the air temperature is fairly warm at sea level. Even without hypothermia, it's good to warm up between snorkels. If you came by car, it will probably be well solar-heated by the time you return.

Sea Urchins

Probably the most common critter injury is stepping on a spiny sea urchin and walking away with lots of spines under your skin. The purple-black spiny sea urchins with long spines tend to appear in groups and favor shallow water, so watch carefully if you see even one. Full-foot flippers or booties help a lot, but don't guarantee protection. Watch where you put your hands – especially in shallow water.

While many folks recommend seeing a doctor for urchin spine slivers, others prefer to just let the spines fester and pop out weeks later. Remove as much spine as you can. Vinegar (or other acidic liquid) will make it feel better. Soaking in Epsom salts helps and the small spines will dissolve in a few weeks, but see a doctor at any sign of infection.

Barracudas

The great barracuda can grow to two meters, has sharp teeth and strong jaws, and swims like a torpedo. For years Judy has removed earrings before swimming after hearing rumors that they attract barracuda, but we've uncovered absolutely no confirming reports of severed ear-ringed ears.

Barracudas are capable of seriously injuring a swimmer so should be taken seriously. Those teeth are just as sharp as they look. Barracudas appear to have attitude, and apparently sometimes do. Our own preference is to respect their territory and allow them some space. Other varieties of barracuda, such as the Heller's (common in schools at 'Ahihi Bay) appear more innocuous.

Once a five-foot great barracuda swam directly beneath us in the Caribbean and appeared annoyed that we were invading his home territory (or so we thought from the fierce look on his face). A calm and steady German surgeon headed up the nearest rocks as if she could fly. The rest of us snorkeled by him repeatedly with no problem, but didn't appreciate the look he gave us. We later came to realize that they always look grumpy, but seldom bite, like some folks you may know. Perhaps the bigger danger comes from eating the delicious barracuda meat, sometimes containing ciguatera, which is toxic to humans.

great barracuda

Portuguese Man-of-War

The Portuguese man-of-war floats on top, looking like a sailfin one to four inches in size, with long stinging filaments that are quite painful. Stay out of the water if you see one. Even avoid dead ones on the sand! They're very pretty in lovely shades of purple, but can cause severe pain.

Vinegar or unseasoned meat tenderizer helps ease the sting and helps stop the release of venom from the stinging cells if tentacles are clinging to you. Use wet sand as a last resort. If you feel ill, see a doctor right away. If jellyfish are present, locals will know which ones are harmful. Jellyfish have seldom been a problem for us in Hawai'i. In all our years in the water in Hawai'i, we've only been stung by a Portuguese man-of-war once.

Rays

Sting rays prefer to avoid you, but hang out on the bottom where they're easy to step on. They prefer resting in calm water that is slightly warmer than the surrounding area –- just the areas favored by people for swimming. Step on them and they may sting you, so the injury is usually to the foot or ankle. They can inflict a serious or painful sting to people – especially children. It's best to get immediate first aid and follow up with medical assistance.

In this case snorkelers have an advantage over swimmers because snorkelers can see sting rays and easily avoid them. In Maui we've seen them swim between children's legs in shallow water at Kapalua Bay and were amazed to see how adept the rays were at avoiding people.

Manta rays don't sting, but they're much larger. Around Maui they are often six to eight feet across weighing several hundred pounds. They maneuver beautifully, so don't pose any danger. With a little luck, you'll be able to see one of these beautiful creatures.

manta ray

Poisonous Fish

Lionfish (also called turkeyfish) and scorpionfish have spines which are very poisonous. Don't step on or touch them! Their poison can cause serious pain and infection or allergic reaction, so definitely see a doctor if you have a close, personal encounter with one. Fins or booties can help protect your tender feet.

Scorpionfish can blend in so well along the bottom in shallow water that they're easy to miss. Turkeyfish, though, are colorful and easy to spot. Since these fish are not abundant in Hawai'i, they are treasured sightings. You are not likely to encounter one in casual snorkeling.

Hawai'ian turkeyfish

Eels

Eels are rarely aggressive and often tamed by divers. Most do possess a formidable array of teeth, which should be avoided. An eel bite can definitely cause serious bleeding requiring prompt medical attention. Another good reason not to snorkel alone!

Eels are fascinating and easy to find in Hawai'i. Count on eels to make every effort to avoid you, so there's no need to panic at the sight of one – even if it's swimming freely. Eels aren't interested in humans as food, but they do want to protect themselves and can usually do so with ease by slipping away into the nearest hole. Do we need to tell you to keep your hands out of crevices in the coral?

leopard moray eel

Cone Shells

The snails inside these pretty black and brown-decorated shells can fire a poisonous dart. The venom can cause a serious reaction or even death – especially to allergic persons. If in doubt, head for a doctor. If you never pick up underwater shells, you won't have any problem.

cone shell

Sharks

Sharks are seldom a problem for snorkelers. In Hawai'i the modest number of verified shark attacks have mostly occurred off O'ahu with tiger sharks the major perpetrator, and surfers the major targets. Sharks often hunt in very murky river runoff, but most snorkelers avoid these conditions anyway.

We have read that you're more likely to be killed by a pig than a shark. We take great comfort in that, as I'm sure you do, too; though we've quit eating bacon just in case.

Some people will suggest you can pet, feed or even tease certain types of shark. We personally would give sharks a bit of respect and leave them entirely in peace. Most sharks are well-fed on fish and not all that interested in well-oiled tourists, but it's hard to tell by looking at a shark whether it has had a bad day.

Sharks usually feed late in the day or at night, causing some people to prefer to enjoy the water more in the morning or midday. If you're in an area frequented by sharks, this might be good to keep in mind. We must admit that we snorkel at any hour, and occasionally night snorkel. The few sharks we have seen have all been midday.

In Maui, with luck, you might possibly see sandbar, black-tip, white-tip or even hammerhead sharks – more often in deep water sites like Molokini.

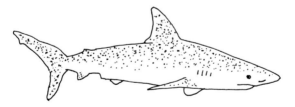

reef shark

I Like to Watch

"For some reason, the barracuda don't seem scary, any more than the ray does. For some reason, none of this seems scary. Even the idea of maybe encountering a smallish s____k doesn't seem altogether bad.

It's beginning to dawn on me that all the fish and eels and crabs and shrimps and plankton who live and work down here are just too busy to be thinking about me.

I'm a traveller from another dimension, not really a part of their already event-filled world, not programmed one way or another–food or yikes–into their instinct circuits. They have important matters to attend to, and they don't care whether I watch or not. And so I watch."

–Dave Barry

Snorkeling Sites

Where are those big beautiful fish?

Maui is justifiably famous as a swimming, sunning and snorkeling destination. Most of the great recreational sites are located on the more protected and relatively dry western side of the island.

For convenient snorkeling, the best areas to stay are West Maui (the Lahaina-Ka'anapali region), Kihei (very central) or the Wailea area (in the southwest). It really isn't a large island, so most sites (apart from the Hana area) are only a short drive if you stay anywhere along the west coast. Other sites are available by boat excursion from boat ramps or Lahaina or Ma'alaea Harbors.

West Maui offers numerous small, pretty bays. Some have large hotels or condos. Others have no facilities at all. Large waves in the winter make snorkeling impossible at some bays in the northern end of West Maui, but other nearby bays shielded from swell can be surprisingly calm on the same day. Kihei, located near flat land where the two mountains have formed a connection, is the most central place to stay. It has convenient access to the highways as well as lower-priced condos and long stretches of sand. While you can see some fish here, there is much better snorkeling not that far away. Kihei's location makes a drive to the north or south quite easy. It doesn't quite have the charm or beauty of some other areas, but is still a good base for exploring the island.

The Wailea/Makena area, south of Kihei, has been growing. Huge new hotels have sprung up like wildflowers (or weeds, depending on whether you're staying there or having to walk through them to get to your favorite beach). Like West Maui, it offers small, undeveloped bays as well as large beaches surrounded by hotels with all amenities. The bays aren't quite as calm as some in the north, but they can be excellent when conditions are good. It can be a bit drier than the north and has some outstandingly beautiful spots.

The entire west coast has plenty of hotels, condos, restaurants, shopping, excursions, hiking, golf and nightlife. The far north and the far south also are very close to some charming, nearly deserted spots. The tall mountains tend to catch most of the rain, so you will usually (but not always) have plenty of sun in these leeward areas. The long stretches of sand are wonderful for lounging, but in Maui, sand is a mixed blessing for snorkelers. Whenever swell rolls in, the sand and sediment gets churned up, making the water a bit murky –

especially after heavy rains, when muddy runoff flows. Don't expect 100 foot visibility, as some brochures imply, along the coast. There's still plenty to see, even with 30-60 foot visibility. Day trips to Molokini Island and Lana'i can take you to clearer waters when you're in the mood.

Maui has small, calm bays with white sandy beaches that are perfect for beginners. Coral, colorful fish, eels, turtle reach – exciting for beginners and experienc More advanced snorkelers can handle lava en around points like Ulua-Mokapu, Makena La

There are countless excursions available to Molokini Island, and Lana'i is just a short boat ride from Lahaina. The channel between these islands is shallow making for a smooth trip most days. Consider taking either the ferry or an excursion to the friendly, uncrowded island of Lana'i, where the snorkeling is excellent. If staying in the south, consider an excursion to the Kanaio Coast.

In the site section ahead, you'll find snorkeling site reviews organized from Maui's far north, proceeding in counter-clockwise direction, with more details about our favorites as well as those with special appeal, such as good beginner beaches. You'll also find details about Molokini Island, as well as the island of Lana'i.

Many sites are surprisingly difficult to find, so bring these maps with you. People often drive up and down the highways with no idea which spots to try for snorkeling. Signs are scarce, so we've included clues and landmarks to help you find your spot.

Whatever your level of swimming or snorkeling ability, you can find a great spot to enjoy yourself along the west coast of Maui. When conditions are right, there are a few other sites farther afield that are worth a try. It's not possible to snorkel all the excellent sites in a week, so we hope that Snorkel Maui and Lana'i will help you select a satisfying sample of the diverse snorkeling opportunities available on Maui and Lana'i

When selecting a site, always consider direction of the swell. If the local paper says 8 foot north swell, stay away from bays that face north. When the swell comes from the south, you might find those northern bays calm as bathwater Conditions can change at any time, so come to Maui prepared to be flexible.

Sites are presented from the northernmost point of Maui following the coast counter-clockwise. Located in the north, the first two sites can be the most difficult. They should be avoided by all but expert snorkelers.

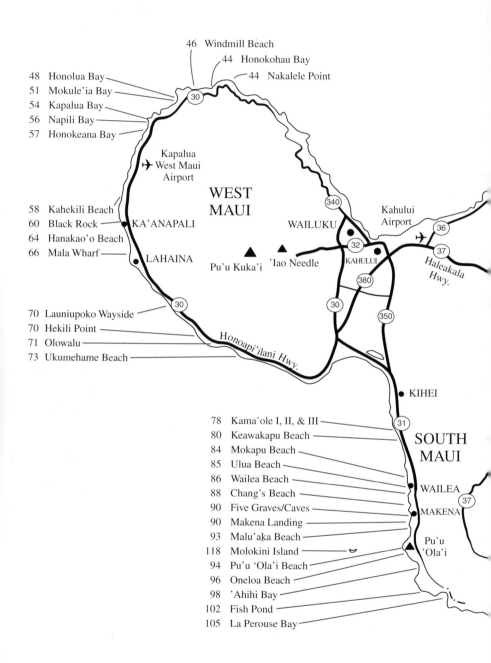

46 Windmill Beach
44 Honokohau Bay
44 Nakalele Point

48 Honolua Bay
51 Mokule'ia Bay
54 Kapalua Bay
56 Napili Bay
57 Honokeana Bay

Kapalua
West Maui
Airport

WEST
MAUI

340

Kahului
Airport

WAILUKU

36

37

58 Kahekili Beach
60 Black Rock
64 Hanakao'o Beach
66 Mala Wharf

KA'ANAPALI

LAHAINA

32

KAHULUI

Haleakala
Hwy.

Pu'u Kuka'i   'Iao Needle

380

30

350

30

30

70 Launiupoko Wayside
70 Hekili Point
71 Olowalu
73 Ukumehame Beach

Honoapi'ilani Hwy.

KIHEI

78 Kama'ole I, II, & III
80 Keawakapu Beach
84 Mokapu Beach
85 Ulua Beach
86 Wailea Beach
88 Chang's Beach
90 Five Graves/Caves
90 Makena Landing
93 Malu'aka Beach
118 Molokini Island
94 Pu'u 'Ola'i Beach
96 Oneloa Beach
98 'Ahihi Bay
102 Fish Pond
105 La Perouse Bay

31

SOUTH
MAUI

WAILEA

37

MAKENA

Pu'u
'Ola'i

38

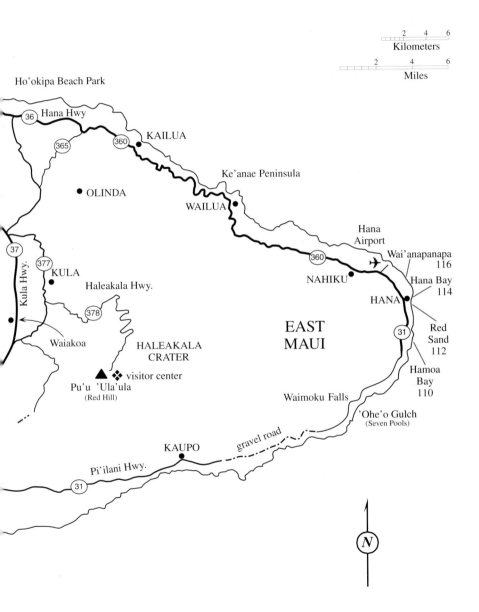

Ho'okipa Beach Park

36 Hana Hwy

365   360   KAILUA

Ke'anae Peninsula

OLINDA

WAILUA

Hana Airport

37

377   360   Wai'anapanapa 116

KULA   NAHIKU   Hana Bay 114

Haleakala Hwy.   HANA

378   Red Sand 112

EAST MAUI

Waiakoa   31

HALEAKALA CRATER   Hamoa Bay 110

visitor center

Pu'u 'Ula'ula   Waimoku Falls

(Red Hill)   'Ohe'o Gulch
(Seven Pools)

gravel road

KAUPO

Pi'ilani Hwy.

31

N

39

Maui Snorkeling Sites at a Glance

	SNORKELING	ENTRY	SANDY BEACH	RESTROOM	SHOWERS	PICNIC AREA	SCENIC	SHADE
Nakalele Point	C	3+					•	
Honokohau Bay	A	2-3				•	•	•
Windmill	C	2	•			•	•	•
Honolua Bay	A	1				•	•	•
Mokule'ia Bay	B	1-3	•			•	•	•
D.T. Fleming Beach	B	3	•	•	•	•	•	•
Oneloa Bay	B	3	•				•	•
Namalu Bay	B	2					•	
Kapalua Bay	A	1	•	•	•	•	•	•
Napili Bay	C	1	•	•	•	•	•	•
Honokeana Bay	A	1-2					•	•
'Alaeloa Bay	B	1	•				•	•
Honokowai	C	2	•	•	•	•	•	
Kahekili	B	1	•	•	•	•	•	•
Black Rock	B	1	•		•		•	
Hanakao'o	B	1-2	•	•	•	•	•	•
Waihikuli	B	1-2	•	•	•	•	•	•
Mala Wharf	B	1-2	•	•	•	•	•	•
Puamana	C	1-2	•	•	•	•	•	•
Launiupoko	B	2	•	•	•	•	•	
Hekili Point	C	1	•					
Olowalu	A	1	•			•	•	
Ukumehame	A	1-2	•			•		
Papalaua	A	1-2	•	•		•	•	
Kalama Beach	C	1-2	•	•	•	•	•	•
Cove Park	C	1-2	•			•	•	•
Charley Young Beach	C	1-2	•	•	•	•	•	•
Kama'ole I, II & III	C	1-2	•	•	•	•	•	•

A	Excellent	1	Easy
B	Good	2	Moderate
C	Fair	3	Difficult

Maui Snorkeling Sites at a Glance

	SNORKELING	ENTRY	SANDY BEACH	RESTROOM	SHOWERS	PICNIC AREA	SCENIC	SHADE
Keawakapu	C	1	•		•	•	•	•
Mokapu Beach	A	1	•	•	•	•	•	•
Ulua Beach	A	1	•	•	•	•	•	•
Wailea Beach	A	1	•	•	•	•	•	•
Polo Beach	B	2	•	•	•	•		•
Chang's Beach	A	1	•	•	•		•	•
Five Graves/Five Caves	A	3					•	•
Makena Landing	A	1	•	•	•	•	•	•
Malu'aka Beach	A	1	•	•	•	•	•	•
Onuoli (Black Sand)	A	1-2	•		•		•	•
Pu'u 'Ola'i (Little) Beach	A	1-2	•				•	•
Oneloa (Big) Beach	C	1-2	•	•		•	•	•
'Ahihi Cove	A	1-2	•				•	•
'Ahihi Bay	A	1-2	•			•	•	•
Fish Pond	A	1	•				•	
'Ahihi-Kina'u	B	1-2					•	
La Perouse Bay	A	3	•			•	•	•
Kanaio Coast	A	1					•	
Hamoa Bay	C	1	•	•	•	•	•	•
Red Sand Beach	A	1-2	•				•	•
Hana Bay	A	1	•	•	•	•	•	•
Wai'anapanapa	B	1-3	•	•	•	•	•	•
Molokini Island	A	1					•	

NOTES

Nakalele Point

On Maui's far northern shore, the winter waves have carved a rugged, but beautiful, landscape of steep cliffs containing arches, tiny coves, tidepools and blow holes. When the weather report predicts north swell, don't even think of swimming here, but on completely calm days, advanced snorkelers could consider this rocky coast. This is the most difficult and dangerous entry we mention, so use extreme caution since there is always the possibility of a rogue wave smearing you like poi finger paint on the rocks. If this happens, don't come crying to us. There are no lifeguards – not to mention, no people at all.

This site is worth the drive for itsbeauty alone, so consider enjoying the dramatic view rather than risking the difficult entry. A spectacular view down to the rugged cliffs can be found by walking down the path straight toward the water. The light station also provides an excellent view, but requires nearly a one-mile hike approaching from the right of the light. In late afternoon you can see lots of turtles grazing along the edge of the rocks directly beneath the light. Nakalele Point offers rugged rock formations, spouts, arches and tidepools. No facilities.

GETTING THERE   Take Highway 30 north past Lahaina and on past Honokohau Bay to Maui's far north. The highway is good, but narrow and winding north of Kapalua. Look for mile marker 38, where you can park on the makai (ocean) side of the highway. The signs here say both "Nakalele Point Light Station" and "Keep Out." Park near the signs and walk along the dirt path toward the light station, which can be seen from the highway (see map, page 45). Walk toward the ironwood trees on the old 4WD road to your right in order to cross the gully and approach the light from the east. To the right of the light station, you may get to see a dramatic blow hole spouting high in the air. When you arrive at the light (after about a mile), you can look down on the area to snorkel. This involves a short, but fairly difficult climb and a risky entry.

Honokohau Bay

This deep, lush valley, sculpted by eons of water runoff from the West Maui Mountains, is a beautiful spot to picnic, swim and snorkel. North swell makes it better for better surfing in the winter months. Facing directly north, deep and narrow, its exposure increases the height of north swell when it arrives each year.

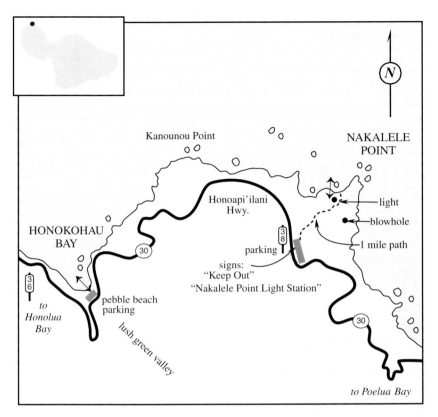

The map shows:
- Kanounou Point
- NAKALELE POINT
- Honoapi'ilani Hwy.
- light
- blowhole
- 1 mile path
- HONOKOHAU BAY
- 30
- parking
- signs: "Keep Out" "Nakalele Point Light Station"
- pebble beach parking
- to Honolua Bay
- lush green valley
- 30
- to Poelua Bay
- N
- 36
- 38

The tiny valley is dramatic and tropical, a small oasis with a number of houses near the bay. Parking is available right along the beach – a beach composed of pebbles rather than sand.

Snorkeling is best along the right side of the bay beyond any breaking waves. Enter carefully to avoid surf as well as small rocks on the bottom. Coral here tends to be quite small due to the rough conditions in winter, but you'll find plenty of interesting fish. Poke around the coral-encrusted large boulders. We saw turtles, a snowflake eel, Christmas wrasses, and a variety of butterflyfish and tangs.

When calm, this is a pretty spot for a swim, although the pebble beach isn't very comfortable on the feet. Once in the water, there's a mostly sandy bottom in the center of the bay. No facilities.

GETTING THERE   Driving north on Highway 30, pass Lahaina, watch for Honolua Bay and continue for another four miles past the Honolua entrance (see map, page 45). Watch for highway marker 36 as the highway drops into Honokohau Valley. You'll easily see the beach and parking area where people often camp.

45

Windmill

Snorkeling is possible at Windmill (named for the steady winds), but it's really too shallow to enjoy – all about one to four feet deep. This is a very popular camping and picnic spot for locals, who like to fish and catch octopus in the shallow, reef-protected area. If you want to snorkel, come at high tide for a little clearance over the reef.

The sign at the highway says "keep out", however the people have been using it as a park for many years, and that seems to be accepted. It's a popular camping and picnic spot. The road down to the beach is well-graded gravel and only about one tenth of a mile. Down at the water you'll find a long grove of ironwood trees, a beautiful view in both directions and a wide mixed pebble and sand beach protected by an outer reef. No facilities are available here. Plenty of parking and shade, so bring a picnic lunch and enjoy.

GETTING THERE   Heading north on Highway 30 past Kapalua, continue until you see mile marker 34. The road down to Windmill is six tenths of a mile beyond this marker. Turn left toward the ocean (makai) on this inconspicuous side road. It leads down to Windmill one-tenth of a mile.

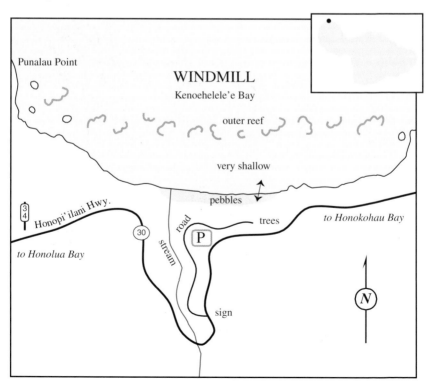

Sign Language

Any serious snorkeler should bother to learn some basic signs starting with some of the standard Scuba ones: OK – meaning "Are you OK?", which should be answered with another "OK", palm up for "stop", wobbling hand for "problem", thumb down meaning "heading down" (in this case referring to surface diving). This is an essential safety issue making it possible to communicate even if slightly separated. See a few of the signs below.

It's also a nuisance to take the snorkel out of your mouth every time you want to say "Did you see that moray?" Worse yet is trying to understand your buddy who frantically gestures and mumbles through the snorkel while you play charades. With a frequent snorkeling companion it's fun to develop signs for the creatures you might see. Eel can be indicated by three fingers looking like an E or by a wavy line drawn in the water. Then all you have to do it point and there it is!

STOP

PROBLEM

OK

GOING DOWN

COLD

SLOWER

47

Honolua Bay

Honolua Bay is half of Honolua-Mokule'ia Bay Marine Life Conservation District. Honolua Bay is the larger bay just to the northeast. In spite of good surfing off the northeastern point, most of Honolua is usually quite well-protected unless winter swells are rolling straight in. Conditions here can change rapidly, so check the weather report.

When calm, Honolua Bay can be like a lake with some of the best snorkeling in Maui. The bay can be murky after heavy rains when the muddy creek water flows into the bay and impairing visibility. From the highway overlook, it's easy to see any muddy water or large swells. On good days, you're likely to see many happy snorkelers exploring the bay.

Park on the highway because the road down to the water is now blocked by a red gate. People may walk around the gate, but should remain on the dirt road that heads to the water. This enjoyable walk is a short stroll through a very beautiful canopied forest that feels like a rain forest jungle. If it has been raining, you will need to ford a small stream – seldom more than a foot deep. If it's deeper you won't want to snorkel anyway because heavy runoff will dump brown water into the bay.

When calm, Honolua Bay is heavenly and has something for everyone, beginner to advanced. You may enter anywhere along the rocky shore, but the easiest spot is in the center, where the dirt road ends (see detail map, page 49). There are remnants of a small old concrete boat ramp at the water's edge. It's sometimes VERY slippery, so you should sit and work your way in slowly. We've often seen people underestimate how slippery concrete or rocks can be at the water's edge, then fall hard when their feet fly into the air.

Snorkeling is excellent on the right side heading towards the point (see detail map, page 49). The center has dramatic deep canyons. We've seen many large fish and turtles there. The left is good too and often calmer, so snorkel all over the bay if time allows and conditions are right. If it's calm enough, snorkel around the point at the left into Mokule'ia Bay, stopping short of the surf line. Be sure to check out all the little coves along the way. It's possible to have a delightful one-way snorkel into Mokule'ia Bay now that a stairway has been built to get you back up to the road. These two bays are close enough for you to walk back on the highway to your car if you've carried along flip-flops or reef shoes and left nothing on shore to retrieve.

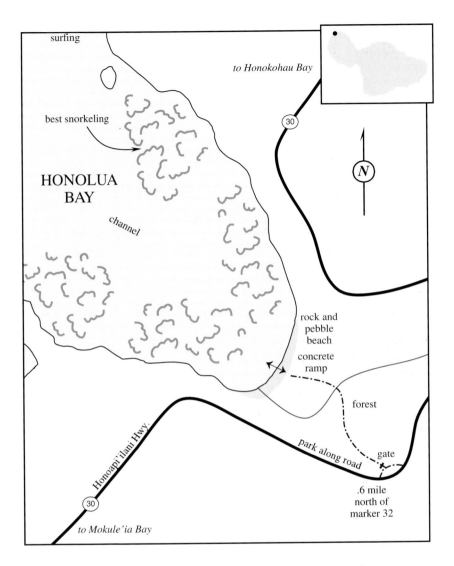

surfing

to Honokohau Bay

best snorkeling

HONOLUA
BAY

channel

30

N

rock and
pebble
beach

concrete
ramp

forest

Honoapi'ilani Hwy.

park along road

gate

.6 mile
north of
marker 32

30

to Mokule'ia Bay

You'll see many large, colorful fish: big chubs greet you, huge tangs, parrot fish, butterflyfish of many kinds, ornate wrasses, scrawled filefish, rectangular triggerfish, lei triggerfish, eels, large turtles, and lots of healthy coral in orange, pink, and light blue. There often are large schools of fish such as blue-stripe snapper or Hawai'ian Flagtails. Stay alert because we've seen an octopus and a white-mouthed moray only ten feet from the concrete ramp entry. This is a beautiful spot for a picnic under deep shade in a jungle setting, but lacks a sandy beach, making it far better for snorkeling than swimming. Don't miss this bay!

Go straight to Honolua when conditions are good. You'll definitely want to return. We've been here when south swell kicked up in the summer. Tourists in the south were despairing of finding a swimmable beach, but Honolua (completely unaffected by south swell) was calm as a bathtub. No facilities here – nearest are at D.T. Fleming Beach Park near Kapalua (see page 52).

GETTING THERE   Head north on Highway 30 past Ka'anapali and Kapalua. Continue past the fence and green railing at Mokule'ia Bay for another half mile to where a dirt road dips down to Honolua Bay (see map, page 50). You can park along the road on the makai (ocean) side either before or after the dirt road with spaces easy to find early in the day. A few minutes walking down the dirt road is easy and beautiful through this miniature rain forest. Rains can quickly cause the creek to rise, so be prepared to wade through if necessary. Reef shoes are handy for this and can save you from injury.

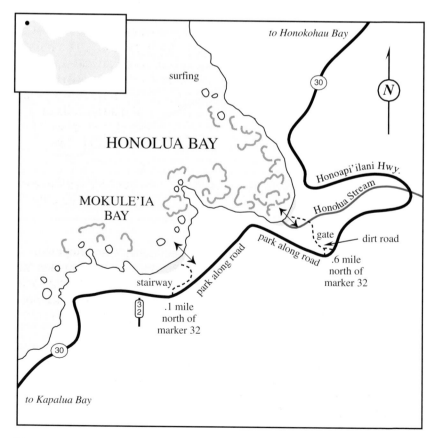

Mokule'ia Bay

Often referred to by its nickname "Slaughterhouse". Mokule'ia Bay is located just southwest of Honolua Bay, and is part of the same marine reserve. A wide, well-built concrete stairway makes access from the highway easy and opens up this pretty bay for picnics, swimming and snorkeling.

This site tends to have rougher surf than Honolua, but has a nice sandy beach, shade trees, good swimming, picnicking and decent snorkeling just beyond the surf on the right. It has less coral and fish with more rubble than Honolua, but can be an excellent spot to see octopus or eel. Check our map on page 50 for the best spots to safely enter and snorkel to the right of the breakers. You will want to watch the swells to be certain it's safe to cross through low surf and arrive at the calm coves beyond. Beginners should stick with Honolua since swells at Mokule'ia can change at any time making an exit more difficult at Mokule'ia. More advanced snorkelers can often safely snorkel around the point into Honolua Bay.

Mokule'ia is a wonderful place with little coves to explore and has sculpted cliffs along the right about halfway to the point. The point to the right is easy to swim around when conditions are calm, so it's hard to resist snorkeling on over to Honolua Bay – or at least to some of the interesting little coves along the way. These two bays are not for any snorkeler when the surf gets heavy. Big swell rolls in often in the winter, and it can get rough any time of year if swell happens to arrive from the north. These bays then become fine surfing sites.

Warning: Unless you are very experienced, snorkel here only in the mornings when quite calm, since waves can pick up unexpectedly and usually get bigger by noon. No facilities.

GETTING THERE   Go north on Highway 30 past Lahaina and Kapalua. Highway marker 31 is at D.T. Fleming Beach. Then watch for marker 32. Go one tenth of a mile past this marker (see map, page 50). Watch for a painted green railing protecting you from the steep cliff. This marks the entrance to the sturdy Mokule'ia Bay stairway. The beach is 88 steps down to the sand.

Parking is only available along the highway and limited to about thirty cars, so come early. You get an excellent view of Molule'ia Bay from the top of the stairs, so check the swells from here. When swells are big, keep driving to Honolua Bay which is usually calmer – especially on the left side.

D.T. Fleming Park (Honokahua Bay)

A popular surfing and picnic spot with wide sand beach, lifeguards, showers, restrooms and picnic tables. There's plenty of reef beyond the breakers, but surf pounds the sand most of the year making it dangerous for snorkelers. Ask the lifeguards before going in the water. When you're heading north, these are the last public facilities.

GETTING THERE   This beach is northeast of the Kapalua area. Take Highway 30 to the first exit past Kapalua and turn left toward the ocean.

Oneloa Bay (Ironwoods)

This large bay (also called Ironwoods) lies west of D.T. Fleming Beach. It has a similar wide sand beach with similar heavy surf most of the year, but supposedly has good snorkeling if you ever find it calm. It seems to catch every swell – we've seen it rough on days when Honolua Bay was flat as a pancake. Don't even think about snorkeling here when waves roll in from the north – which is common in the winter. Water faucet on the left of the path. No facilities.

GETTING THERE   This is the next beach NE of Kapalua (see map, page 53). Turn toward the water at Ironwood Lane. You will immediately see a small public parking lot ("beach users only") before the gate. Take the marked concrete public access path down stairs to the sand.

Namalu Bay

Just north of Kapalua Bay and directly in front of the Kapalua Bay Resort, you'll find a small, pretty bay lined with rocks. It has good snorkeling, although not quite as good as Kapalua. The rocky entry is very slippery and the water tends to be a bit choppy, so most snorkelers will prefer Kapalua Bay. If you're curious and conditions are calm, give uncrowded Namalu a try. When it's calm, good swimmers can snorkel around the point at the left to Kapalua Bay.

GETTING THERE   Park in the public parking area for Kapalua Bay (access #219), walk down the steps and through the tunnel to the right. Continue on the path to the far side of broad Kapalua Beach. From the end of the beach it's just a short walk of about 100 yards through the hotel grounds to cross the point (see map, page 53).

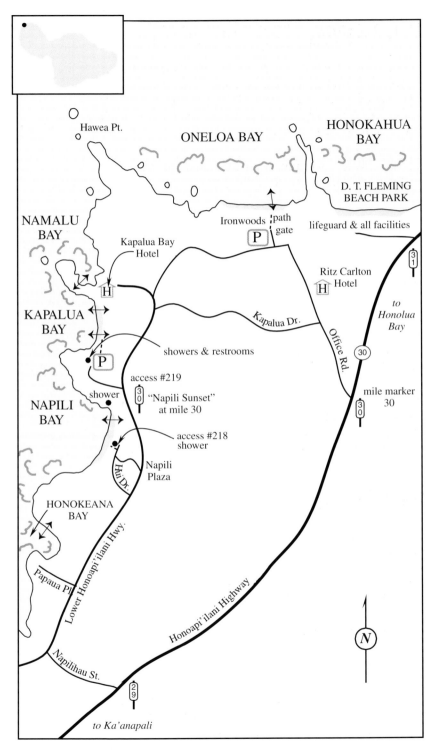

Hawea Pt.

ONELOA BAY

HONOKAHUA BAY

D. T. FLEMING BEACH PARK

NAMALU BAY

Ironwoods

path gate

lifeguard & all facilities

P

Kapalua Bay Hotel

Ritz Carlton Hotel

H

to Honolua Bay

H

KAPALUA BAY

Kapalua Dr.

Office Rd.

30

31

showers & restrooms

P

access #219

"Napili Sunset" at mile 30

mile marker 30

30

shower

3 0

NAPILI BAY

access #218 shower

Hui Dr.

Napili Plaza

HONOKEANA BAY

Lower Honoapi'ilani Hwy.

Papaua Pl.

Honoapi'ilani Highway

N

Napilihau St.

2 9

to Ka'anapali

Kapalua Bay

This popular postcard-perfect beach just south of the Kapalua Bay Resort has good snorkeling and easy entry anywhere along its lovely crescent of sand – making it an excellent choice for beginners. This resort is a great location for snorkelers since it provides relatively calm swimming and snorkeling as well as quick access (five minutes by car) to superb northern sites such as Honolua Bay.

The best snorkeling at Kapalua Bay is on the right as far as the point, although the whole bay is interesting: left, center and even close to shore. When the surf kicks up along the west coast, try heading here because it's usually as calm as Maui gets. Public parking is limited to about 25 cars and the lot fills early. There is no alternative parking available anywhere close.

Kapalua Bay tends to stay calm and the crowds ease after noon. Showers and restrooms are available on the beach side of the public parking lot. Once you find a parking space, the path to the beach is short – down a few steps, through a tunnel and there's the beach!

The bay is small, so you can swim around the whole area if you wish. We have seen eels, a turtle, an octopus, as well as most of the many colorful fish that call Maui home. When calm enough, a strong swimmer can snorkel around the point to the left and end up at Napili Bay – only a short hike back to your car if you cut through the condo developments. If you decide to try this, the best place to exit is the sandy corner near the shower (see map, page 192).

GETTING THERE   Kapalua Bay has just one public access, #219 (see map, page 55). Look sharp, since it's easy to miss the tiny blue access sign. Parking fills up early, but often has plenty of space later in the afternoon. Drive north on Highway 30, past Ka'anapali and take the next major Y to the left, which is Lower Honoapi'ilani Road. Following the coast, just one tenth of a mile north of marker 30, you'll see the Napili Kai Beach Club on your left and a tiny blue beach access sign on the right. Turn left here and park in the public lot at the end of the road on the right. You'll see the showers and restrooms toward the beach. To the right of the restrooms, follow the path down steps into a tunnel. Entry to the bay is usually easy anywhere along the sandy beach.

Or take Highway 30 north and turn left on Napilihau Street. Then turn right on Lower Honoapi'ilani Road. Watch for mile marker 30 and you'll find the blue access sign just one-tenth of a mile to the north. Turn left here at the Napili Kai Beach Club.

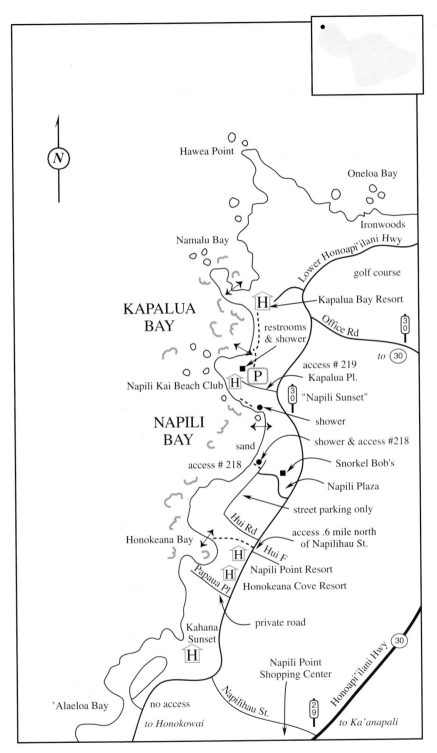

Hawea Point

Oneloa Bay

Ironwoods

Lower Honoapi'ilani Hwy

golf course

Namalu Bay

Kapalua Bay Resort

Office Rd

KAPALUA
BAY

to (30)

restrooms
& shower

access # 219
Kapalua Pl.

Napili Kai Beach Club

"Napili Sunset"

shower

NAPILI
BAY

shower & access #218

sand

Snorkel Bob's

access # 218

Napili Plaza

street parking only

access .6 mile north
of Napilihau St.

Hui Rd

Honokeana Bay

Hui F

Napili Point Resort

Papaua Pl

Honokeana Cove Resort

private road

Kahana
Sunset

Napili Point
Shopping Center

Honoapi'ilani Hwy (30)

'Alaeloa Bay

no access

to Honokowai

Napilihau St.

to Ka'anapali

Napili Bay

Much larger than Kapalua Bay, this next bay to the south offers some snorkeling on the right side. It's a beautiful place to picnic, swim, sun or snorkel. Napili Bay is completely surrounded by condos, so there are often plenty of people here enjoying the sandy beach. If you want to snorkel, try to park at the far north because it's a long walk across the beach otherwise.

Entry is easy from the sand, but you can also enter from the rocks in several places from the path in front of the condos along the right point. Although Napili Bay has three public accesses, there is very little parking available along the street, so come early in the morning or later in the afternoon.

Unfortunately, brown algae and sand has covered much of the reef in recent years making for disappointing snorkeling. A small simple shower is available along the public access path #218, but the nearest public restrooms are located at the Kapalua parking lot (access #219).

GETTING THERE   Napili has two public beach access signs, but both are easy to miss, and neither offers much parking (see map, page 55). Going north on Highway 30 past Ka'anapali, turn left at the Napili exit (Napilihau St.). Turn right when it hits Lower Honoapi'ilani Rd. and continue to the north (right) past 'Alaeloa.

When you see signs for the various Napili condos, watch for little blue beach access signs. Each offers a bit of on-street parking. Access point #219 is the furthest north, so using it gets you closer to the snorkeling. Walk to the left instead of the right (Kapalua Bay is to the right). There is a small shower tucked away at the corner of the beach along the walkway in front of the condos.

Access point #218 is hidden (see map, page 55) behind a small shopping center (Napili Plaza) on Lower Honoapi'ilani. Just continue driving through the shopping center toward the water past Snorkel Bob's (ignoring the warning sign) and there is access #218! You'll even find a small public shower along this short path to the water.

From Lower Honoapi'ilani (heading north) you can also take a left on little Hui Road to get to this access. There are a handful of parking spaces along Hui Rd., available if you arrive early in the morning or later in the afternoon. All of the Napili parking is on the street unless you use the Kapalua lot.

Honokeana Bay

This hidden little bay offers great snorkeling and typically calm water, but it's hard to find. When conditions are rough elsewhere, you might consider trying Honokeana. What you'll find is a pretty bay surrounded by condos perched on small hills overlooking the bay. There is no beach to speak of, so entry is from lava on the north side of the bay through Napili Shores Resort. The whole bay is well-protected by an outer reef and is about the perfect depth for good snorkeling (three to ten feet). We saw turtles, lots of rectangular triggerfish, teardrop and raccoon butterflyfish, unicornfish and more. On a calm day it's easy to snorkel beyond the points as well.

Honokeana Bay is excellent for beginners providing you walk carefully across the lava. There's enough here to keep any snorkeler happy. Be sure to check it out – especially if conditions aren't too calm elsewhere. Honokeana Bay is well-sheltered from swells as well as from wind.

GETTING THERE   Heading north on Highway 30, turn left at the Napili exit (Napilihau St.). Then turn right when you get to Lower Honoapi'ilani (see map, page 55). Pass Papalua Place. on your left and watch for Napili Point Resort. Park along the street and walk through the parking lot just north of the resort and before Da Store. About 2/3 of the way through the parking lot, go left between the buildings. You will immediately see a lovely bay on the other side. Enter from the lava rocks directly in front of you – assuming the bay is calm.

'Alaeloa

This charming little beach, without much sand, looks like it could have good snorkeling with space to explore from a pebbled entry. Getting to the beach is the main problem, since the only land access is across private property. The surrounding development has a gate and the houses are rented on a monthly basis, so it isn't easy to gain entrance. This development went in before public access was required and they seem quite determined to keep it private.

GETTING THERE   Finding 'Alaeloa is easy (see map, page 55). There's only one way in with a prominent sign on Lower Honoapi'ilani Road. This gate is the only entrance. It would be a long swim from any other bay. A boat could drop you off and pick you up later or you might kayak in. The beach itself belongs to the public according to Hawai'ian law.

Honokowai Park

The reef here is very shallow, making swimming difficult and a bit hazardous at times. At low tide, however, there are tide pools perfect for young children. To get beyond the shallow part, swim out at the far north of the park (to your right). Only the ocean side of the reef is deep enough for snorkeling, so go on a very calm day at high tide. This is not a good place for beginners. You'll find a shady, grassy park with picnic tables, facilities, and a store right across the street in case you forgot to bring a picnic.

GETTING THERE   This park is easy to spot along Lower Honoapi'ilani Road and has plenty of parking. Going north from Ka'anapali on Highway 30, angle left on Lower Honoapi'ilani Road and watch for the first beach makai (ocean side). You'll find the park across the street from the small market. On the ocean side you will see a square grassy area with shade trees, picnic tables, restrooms and shower.

Kahekili (Old Airport)

This pleasant beach park is popular with locals and divers, but easy to miss. With a gentle sandy beach, it's a nice spot for beginners and usually quite calm. It is often called Old Airport Beach because it's near the former site of the West Maui Airport.

We prefer to snorkel to the right from the northern boundary of the park (see map, page 192). The reef here is easy to find, near shore and just about the perfect depth (three to ten feet deep). The snorkeling area runs for about a mile north offering a chance to wander and enjoy. While not spectacular, the coral and fish are interesting if you take the time to watch carefully. Beginners who find Olowalu too shallow for comfort will like the extra clearance at Kahekili.

We were trailed by hungry unicornfish looking for a handout. We also saw groups of raccoon butterflyfish, several eels, an octopus, and even turtles. The coral is pretty and healthy, but not very large. Kahekili is open from 6:00 a.m. until half an hour after sunset. It has restrooms, a shower, shade trees, grass, picnic tables, barbecue grills and an ample parking lot.

More advanced snorkelers may want to snorkel a half mile to the north. When a slow current runs south, swim against it as far as comfortable, then catch a faster ride back to the park. You're always close to shore with an easy exit anywhere along the way.

GETTING THERE   Go north on Highway 30 until the last exit for Ka'anapali (see map, page 59). This intersection is called Kai Ala Drive on the ocean side (makai) and Pu'ukali'i Road towards the mountains (mauka). Turn left toward the ocean and angle right into the parking lot rather than left to the Maui Ka'anapali Villas. You'll find plenty of parking and most of it in the shade.

Kahekili is across the highway from a Sugar Train station, so you can snorkel to train sounds in the background as well as planes flying directly overhead as they approach the Kapalua Airport.

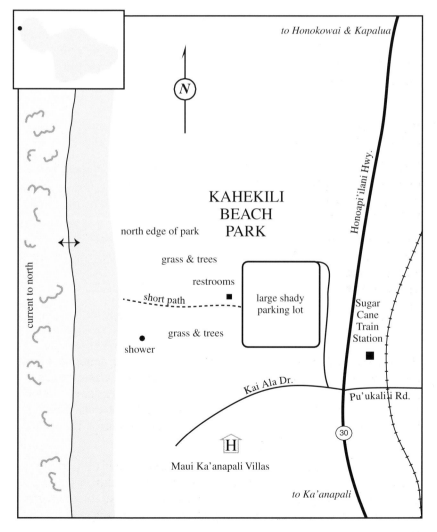

Black Rock (Keka'a Point)

The ever-popular point occupied by the Sheraton offers fairly good snorkeling, though it is modestly endowed with coral and fish. This is a pretty enough spot to make it worth your while finding a parking spot – the major challenge. Shoreline access #213 (see map, page 192) is located between the Sheraton Maui and the Ka'anapali Beach Hotel. The access sign and path are easy to find, but parking is quite another matter. The Sheraton provides a small corner of its parking structure for the public. Check our map, then come early (before 9 a.m.) to nab one of the twenty spaces. Otherwise you will have to wait for someone to leave, park illegally or pay to park at Whaler's Village.

From the sand, head to the north end of the beach and snorkel along the rocky cliff as far as it's calm. Often you can round the point, stopping to explore nooks and crannies along the way. Beginners should stay where the water is flat, but experienced snorkelers can easily swim all the way around the point when the water is calm.

While there isn't much coral here, the fish are varied and somewhat tame, so there's plenty to see. We enjoyed watching a bold octopus near the point, saw a couple of spotted eagle rays cruising the point, as well as a variety of tangs, triggerfish, needlefish and cornetfish. Watch for pairs of several kinds of butterflyfish such as the teardrop and the beautiful oval. Watch closely. We saw the octopus in about five feet of water, but all the other snorkelers zipped on past without spotting it.

There are no public facilities here, but the big hotels have showers at the edge of the sand.

GETTING THERE   Heading north past Lahaina on Highway 30, take the main Ka'anapali turnoff called Ka'anapali Parkway (see map, page 61). Follow the Parkway to the right toward the Sheraton. On this divided road continue slowly until you see the sign for the public access path just before the parking garage. You'll have to continue a bit further on this divided road until you can make a U-turn. The public parking entrance is easy to miss. It's located in the southern corner of the Sheraton garage, which is next to the public access path.

When these spaces are filled, you might find a spot further south at any of several beach access parking areas (marked on our map). A walkway on the ocean side of the hotels will get you to Black Rock, but it can be a long hike. Whaler's Village has a pay parking lot.

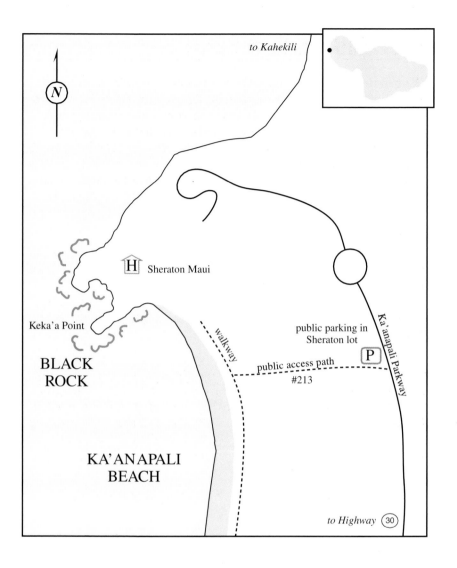

to Kahekili

N

Sheraton Maui

Keka'a Point

BLACK
ROCK

walkway

public parking in
Sheraton lot

P

public access path
#213

Ka'anapali Parkway

KA'ANAPALI
BEACH

to Highway 30

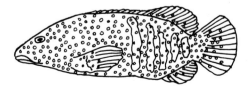

peacock grouper

Ka'anapali Beach

Ka'anapali Beach, other than Black Rock, is better for swimming and people watching than snorkeling. People are starting to call it DigMe Beach because it's THE place to see and be seen. If you're not staying at a local hotel, you'll need to find a parking space before you can start socializing.

GETTING THERE   There are four more public access paths (with parking) along the rest of Ka'anapali. Heading north on Highway 30, take the main exit called Ka'anapali Parkway, then turn left at the hotels.

The first public access going south is #212 just south of Whaler's Village (see map, page 63). There are about 50 designated, but scattered spaces in this parking lot and the path is found just to the south of the parking lot.

The next public access is #211 between the Westin and the Ka'anapali Ali'i. It's easy to miss, doesn't have obvious parking, and provides a 200-yard path to the sand.

Access #210 has ten parking spaces and is located between the Ka'anapali Ali'i and the Marriott. The path is just to the south of parking.

Access #209 provides about 25 spaces and is found between the Marriott and the Hyatt. Again, the path is just south of the public parking.

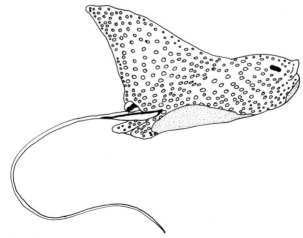

spotted eagle ray

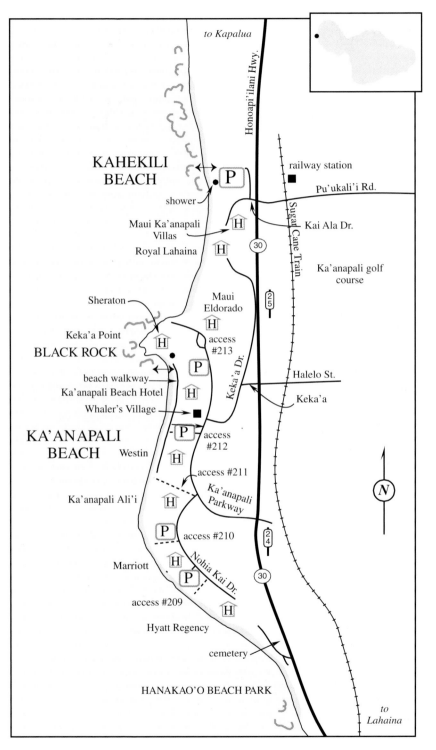

to Kapalua

Honoapi'ilani Hwy.

KAHEKILI
BEACH

shower

railway station

Pu'ukali'i Rd.

Maui Ka'anapali
Villas

Royal Lahaina

Kai Ala Dr.

Sugar Cane Train

30

Ka'anapali golf
course

Maui
Eldorado

Sheraton

Keka'a Point
BLACK ROCK

access
#213

2
5

beach walkway
Ka'anapali Beach Hotel
Whaler's Village

Keka'a Dr.

Halelo St.

Keka'a

KA'ANAPALI
BEACH

Westin

access
#212

Ka'anapali Ali'i

access #211

Ka'anapali
Parkway

access #210

Marriott

Nohia Kai Dr.

2
4

30

access #209

Hyatt Regency

cemetery

N

HANAKAO'O BEACH PARK

to
Lahaina

63

Hanakao'o Beach Park (Cemetery)

Located south of Ka'anapali, stretching along Highway 30 starting at Hanakao'o Cemetery in the north, giving it the nickname Cemetery. Lots of parking, lifeguards, restrooms, shower, grass and shade trees. Park as far south as possible to enter from a sandy beach. While surfers wait for waves directly in front of the lifeguard station, the area south of the park offers good snorkeling and is usually calm. We like to enter from the sand and snorkel south to the next park. This takes you through plenty of interesting coral and fish. When calm, it's an easy shallow snorkel – with comfortable depth (five to ten feet). Don't worry if you pass a great barracuda looking mean and territorial. We also have seen some large bluespine unicornfish, big schools of goat fish, and colorful coral – lavender, green, yellow, orange and pink. The snorkeling spot we like best is across from the culvert halfway between Hanakao'o and Waihikuli parks (see map, page 192).

In calm weather, this is a good site for beginners with easy entry from sand, good depth and not far from shore. You will definitely want to enter and exit from the sand rather than the lava.

GETTING THERE   From Lahaina, go north on Highway 30 watching for mile marker 23 (near the post office and county buildings mauka). Continue north to the next beach park on your left (see map, page 65).

From Ka'anapali, head south on Highway 30. The park entrance is half a mile south of Ka'anapali Parkway. Turn toward the water, then left to park in the southernmost parking lot for easy access to the beach.

Waihikuli Beach Park

This narrow strip along the makai (ocean) side of Highway 30 offers parking, picnic tables, grass and shade. Most of the coast is rocky here, so entry is from the tiny bits of sandy beach. Small, scattered parking areas are visible from the highway. While you can snorkel here, conditions are better further south or north.

Experienced snorkelers might want to enter the water here for a one-way snorkel to Hanakao'o Beach Park (the next beach to the north). Entry is easier at Hanakao'o, but the good snorkeling is about halfway in between (see map, page 65). Waihikuli and Hanaka'o'o are about half a mile apart.

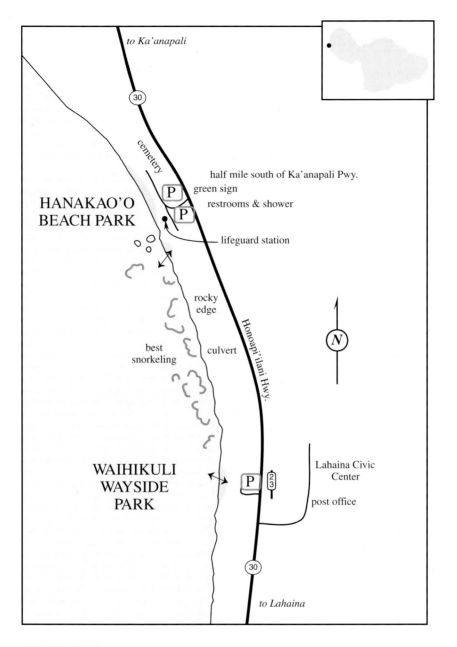

to Ka'anapali

30

cemetery

half mile south of Ka'anapali Pwy.

HANAKAO'O
BEACH PARK

P

green sign

P

restrooms & shower

lifeguard station

rocky
edge

Honoapi'ilani Hwy.

best
snorkeling

culvert

N

WAIHIKULI
WAYSIDE
PARK

P

2
3

Lahaina Civic
Center

post office

30

to Lahaina

GETTING THERE Heading north on Highway 30 from Olowalu, watch for highway marker 23 just after the turnoff on your right for the Lahaina Civic Center (see map, page 65). At marker 23, turn left toward the ocean to enter the park. Enter the water at the sandy beach and snorkel north for the best snorkeling. Our favorite spot here is about a quarter mile north and close to the shore.

Mala Wharf

This site offers better snorkeling than it might appear. There's enough parking and a steep sandy beach just south of the old pier. When the beach is calm, you can enter easily and snorkel near the pier to watch for baby sharks. To see turtles, head straight out to sea where you're sure to see them in the twenty-foot deep water. Excursions sometimes stop here after a day in Lana'i.

GETTING THERE   From Lahaina, head north on Front St. (see map, page 66) until you see the signs to Mala Wharf. There is beach access and parking from Ala Moana St.

From north of Lahaina, take Highway 30 south to Front St. Watch on the ocean side for the Mala Wharf and beach access signs on Ala Moana.

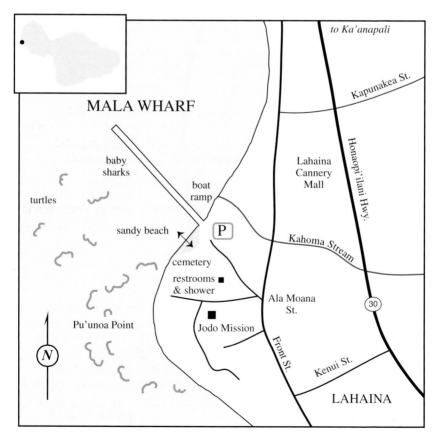

Lahaina

While there is coral along the shore of the city of Lahaina, most of the area is usually rough and lacks much in the way of sand – making it better for surfing. Snorkeling is better at Mala Wharf at the north end of town or Puamana in the south.

Street parking is mostly restricted to two hours, but small parking lots for pay are available scattered throughout the center of the city. These lots charge $6 for all-day parking.

South of the city center, you'll find three public access paths to areas where there is sand as well as some snorkeling, although not the best.

GETTING THERE   Heading south on Front St. from the center of Lahaina, watch for the little blue public access signs. Just past Lahaina Shores you'll see access #203, a gravel path that goes fifty yards to the sand. Next south comes access #202 with a forty-yard concrete walkway. Just before Puamana, access #201 provides a twenty-yard path to the sand.

Puamana Beach Park

This little park is located just south of the housing area called Puamana. It has a sand beach, portapotties and picnic tables. While it's possible to snorkel here on a calm day, both swimming and snorkeling are better at most nearby parks. This one is best for surfing and picnics.

GETTING THERE   Going south on Highway 30 from Lahaina, Puamana is the first park just south of Lahaina. There's parking and a small beach – on the makai (ocean) side of Highway 30.

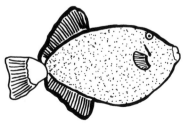

pinktail triggerfish

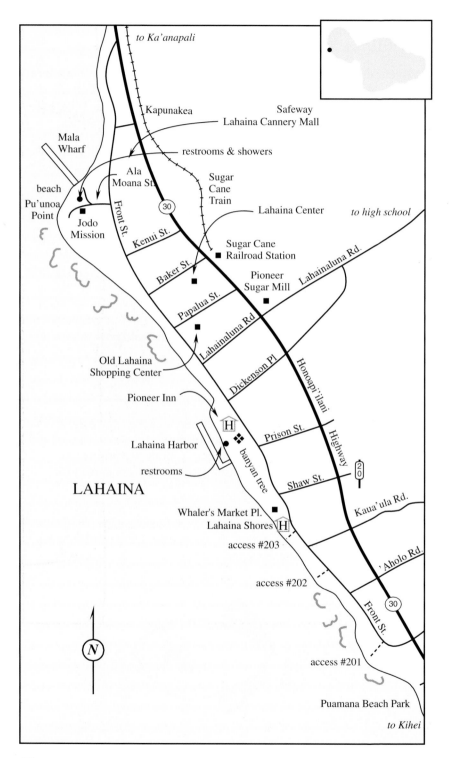

to Ka'anapali

Kapunakea

Safeway
Lahaina Cannery Mall

Mala
Wharf

restrooms & showers

Ala
Moana St.

Sugar
Cane
Train

beach
Pu'unoa
Point

Lahaina Center

to high school

Front St.

30

Jodo
Mission

Kenui St.

Sugar Cane
Railroad Station

Lahainaluna Rd.

Baker St.

Pioneer
Sugar Mill

Lahainaluna Rd

Papalua St.

Lahainaluna Rd

Dickenson Pl

Honoapi'ilani

Old Lahaina
Shopping Center

Pioneer Inn

H

Prison St.

Highway

Lahaina Harbor

banyan tree

20

restrooms

LAHAINA

Shaw St.

Whaler's Market Pl.
Lahaina Shores

H

Kaua'ula Rd.

access #203

access #202

'Aholo Rd.

30

Front St.

N

access #201

Puamana Beach Park

to Kihei

68

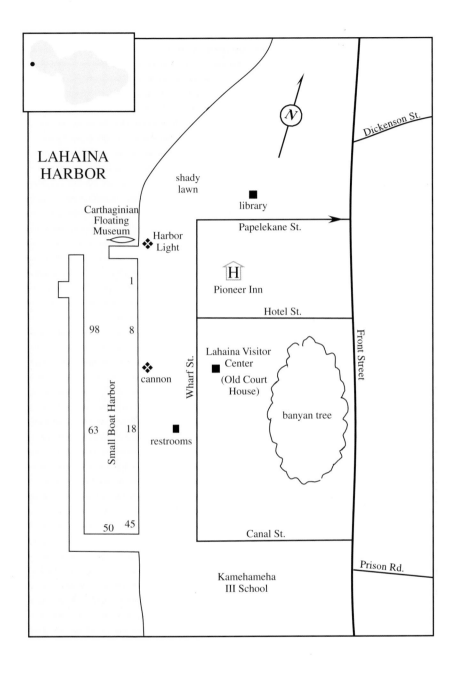

LAHAINA
HARBOR

N

Dickenson St.

shady
lawn

library

Carthaginian
Floating
Museum

Papelekane St.

Harbor
Light

H
Pioneer Inn

Hotel St.

1

Lahaina Visitor
Center
(Old Court
House)

Front Street

98   8

banyan tree

cannon

Wharf St.

Small Boat Harbor

63   18

restrooms

50   45

Canal St.

Prison Rd.

Kamehameha
III School

Launiupoko County Wayside

Just north of mile marker 18 on Highway 30 you'll find this popular beach park. The waves are usually big enough for surfing, but a shallow kiddie pool is formed by the breakwater at the center of the park. You'll find lots of grass, parking, restrooms, showers, picnic tables, shade trees and a little sand. The calm beach is at the south end of the park, so that's the spot to enter for some modest snorkeling. Picnicking here is the main attraction.

GETTING THERE Between Lahaina and Olowalu, this park is located along the ocean side of Highway 30, one tenth of a mile north of mile marker 18 (see map, page 73). You'll see Kaiheleku St. heading toward the new housing in the foothills opposite the park. Turn into the park and look for a parking spot as far south as possible to be near the sandy area. Directly in front of the park the waves are more suited to surfing.

Hekili Point

This certainly isn't nearly as rich a snorkeling spot as nearby Olowalu, but is calm, shallow and easy. It also offers a chance to study small fish and small coral heads. There's actually plenty going on in this shallow area. You can view the rice coral where beautiful green-eyed boxfish hang out. Watch the sandy bottom for the well-disguised octopus or flounder. You'll also see plenty of tiny versions of your favorite fish since this shallow area (less than five feet deep within the protected area) is a good fish nursery.

GETTING THERE On Highway 30 watch for the Olowalu General Store and mile marker 15 (see map, page 71), and turn toward the ocean right across from the store. Then take an immediate left rather than straight into private property. Follow this dirt road as it curves back toward the ocean and soon dead-ends in the small dirt parking area. A short path takes you to the ocean where you can see an old wharf to the left of the breakwater. Between them is a tiny sandy boat launching corridor where you can enter the water with ease. There are no facilities here.

Snorkel to the left anywhere within the protecting outer reef. It's an interesting opportunity to see juvenile fish – some exact scaled-down replicas of their parents, others with wildly different markings and shapes.

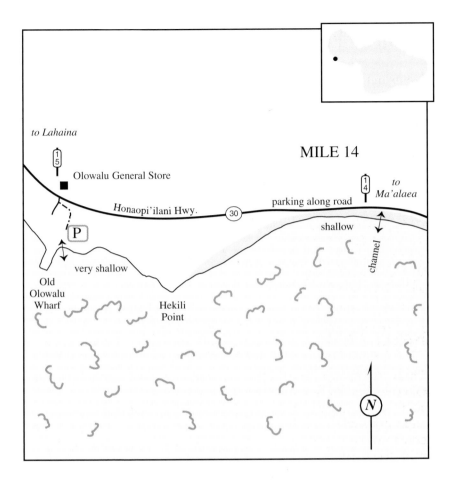

Olowalu Beach (Mile 14)

Olowalu Beach is a very long beach with good snorkeling almost anywhere. The most famous spot is called Mile 14, since it's near that highway marker. This large, almost always calm, easy snorkeling area has something for everyone. Its long stretch of soft white sand has plenty of shade trees, parking and easy entry points. Beginners and children can stay close to shore if they wish.

Better snorkelers can weave around the extensive reefs for about a mile straight out to sea, left or right. The coral here is large and mostly quite healthy. There's plenty to see in every direction and it could hardly be easier as long as it is calm – which is almost year round, because the reef extends far out to sea and offers protection from the surf. At this site, parking is no problem at all. You'll see cars parked along the highway the whole length of the beach.

You don't need to limit yourself to snorkeling out the main channel noted on the map, unless you're concerned about having a twenty-foot wide channel to head out through the coral, or the tide is low. There are plenty of passages through the reef and you can safely swim over most of the coral unless the tide is unusually low or the swell is high. When the sea is calm, even a beginner would have no problem finding an easy passage. If you like plenty of clearance, just arrive near high tide.

We've been to Olowalu when it was clear near shore, but other times visibility was less than five feet. Brown algae can sometimes make for poor snorkeling near shore, as it covers up and crowds out the coral. Clean, healthy coral and visibility increase as you head out toward the outer, deeper reef. Experienced snorkelers can swim nearly a mile to what is called the Olowalu Outer Reef – assuming calm conditions. Beginners will enjoy getting beyond the first section of reef just to marvel at the size of the coral.

This entire snorkeling area has coral 3-25 feet below the surface. You will see dramatic formations with large coral heads. Watch for most of Hawai'i's varied butterflyfish (lots of pairs of pretty ovals, teardrops and ornates). We have seen plenty of colorful parrotfish, groups of raccoon butterflyfish lined up in a row, turtles, cornetfish, boxfish with green eyes and more.

This is a pretty picnic spot and great for small children who just want to splash in the calm water. Since the reef is so close to shore, this isn't the best spot for barefoot swimming. No facilities are located here. For restrooms, drive south to Ukumehame Beach Park.

GETTING THERE   Just south of the Olowalu General Store near mile marker 14 is an extensive area for snorkeling (see map, page 71). There's plenty of parking on the makai (ocean) side of the highway, with shade available. You'll see clusters of cars at popular spots. You might want to try the center first, then return another day to explore this exceptionally broad reef area. The wide channel is located about fifty feet south of marker 14 and appears light green in contrast to the darker reef area.

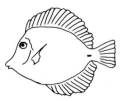

yellow tang

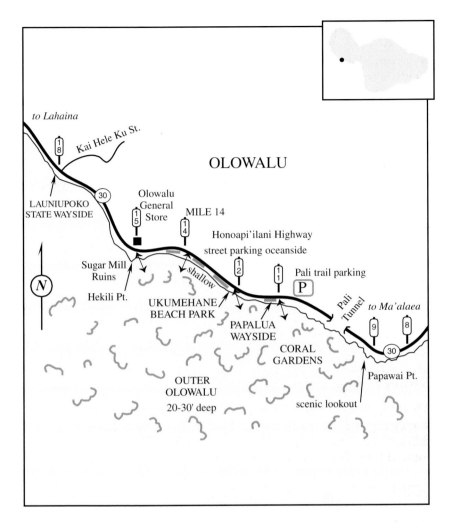

to Lahaina

Kai Hele Ku St.

OLOWALU

LAUNIUPOKO STATE WAYSIDE

Olowalu General Store

MILE 14

Honoapi'ilani Highway

street parking oceanside

Sugar Mill Ruins

shallow

Pali trail parking

Hekili Pt.

P

UKUMEHANE BEACH PARK

to Ma'alaea

PAPALUA WAYSIDE

CORAL GARDENS

Papawai Pt.

OUTER OLOWALU

20-30' deep

scenic lookout

N

Pali Tunnel

Ukumehame Beach Park

This small beach park south of Olowalu is slightly less protected, so not as calm. It has a sandy beach, but appears rather shallow and rocky for comfortable snorkeling. It also tends to catch more of the wind. It does have portable toilets which nearby snorkeling sites lack.

GETTING THERE   Between Olowalu and Papalaua on Highway 30, you'll see this park right by the highway on the makai (ocean) side (see map, page 73). It's between mile markers 12 and 13.

73

Papalaua Wayside Park (Coral Gardens)

Just south of Ukumehame is another of the small parks along the makai (ocean) side of Highway 30 between Olowalu and the Pali Tunnel. Located at mile marker 11, it provides a good entry point for snorkeling Coral Gardens, a popular snorkeling boat destination. The best spot to enter is from the small sandy beach at the south end of the park. Snorkel out to sea and toward the south to see the area called Coral Gardens (see map, page 192). When the sea is calm, snorkel about 300 yards from shore to see large coral heads spread over a wide area. The reef is 3-15 feet deep all the way making for good viewing. Our favorite spot is directly out to sea from the trail head marked on our map.

Coral Gardens can also be reached from the highway further south – from the Lahaina Pali Trail parking area across the highway, but there isn't a sandy entry here, just rocky shore. There are no facilities here other than portable toilets and parking.

GETTING THERE   When we last snorkeled here, the park had no sign, so watch for mile markers to know which of the little seaside parks will access Coral Gardens (see map, page 73).

From Lahaina go south on Highway 30 until you see mile marker 11. This is six tenths of a mile north of the Pali Tunnel. Park at the southern end of the park and enter from the sandy beach, swimming out and south to explore this extensive reef.

From Kihei head north to Highway 30. After emerging from the Pali Tunnel, drive six tenths of a mile more to the little park on the makai (ocean) side of the highway.

Picasso triggerfish

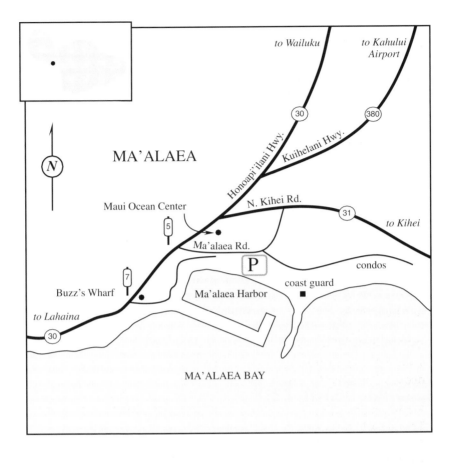

to Wailuku

to Kahului Airport

MA'ALAEA

N

30

380

Honoapi'ilani Hwy.

Kuihelani Hwy.

N. Kihei Rd.

Maui Ocean Center

5

31

to Kihei

Ma'alaea Rd.

P

condos

7

coast guard

Buzz's Wharf

Ma'alaea Harbor

to Lahaina

30

MA'ALAEA BAY

rectangular triggerfish

Kihei Beaches

The Kihei area offers plenty of condos and plenty of sand (see map, page 61). While this isn't the best area to snorkel, the pretty beach is about six miles long, so there's ample room to swim and sun. Most of the beaches can be seen as you travel south on Kihei Road. They usually have good public facilities including parking, restrooms and showers.

The town itself has markets, shopping, banks and restaurants. This can be a cooler part of Maui in the summer because the winds often blow across this low area between Maui's high mountains. Kihei offers a wide range of condos (some very inexpensive) and the area is convenient for excursions around the island, so it's not a bad base for snorkelers as long as you don't expect to snorkel in Kihei all the time. We prefer to be located a bit outside the town to avoid the crowds. The long stretches of sand and fairly calm water make this a popular spot for families with young children. While the center of town is somewhat crowded, the condos at each end of town (especially north toward Ma'alaea) are often very quiet.

Kalama Beach Park

This large popular park has room for everyone and is often calm enough for safe swimming and a bit of snorkeling. There's plenty of parking, grass, soft sand, restrooms and picnic tables, however, not really much to see underwater. Still, when calm, it's a good place to learn how to snorkel. It's also a good spot for children with a play area, shallow water and plenty of space to run around.

GETTING THERE   Located in the center of Kihei along South Kihei Road, this large park is easy to find. From Highway 31, take the Lipoa exit (see map, page 77) and continue south on S. Kihei Road.

needlefish

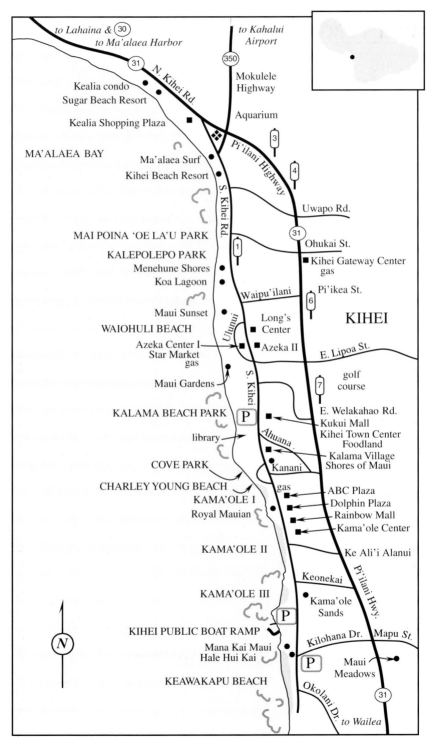

to Lahaina & (30)
to Ma'alaea Harbor

to Kahalui
Airport

(31)

N. Kihei Rd

(350)

Mokulele
Highway

Kealia condo
Sugar Beach Resort

Kealia Shopping Plaza

Aquarium

Pi'ilani Highway

3

MA'ALAEA BAY

Ma'alaea Surf
Kihei Beach Resort

S. Kihei Rd.

4

Uwapo Rd.

(31)

Ohukai St.

MAI POINA 'OE LA'U PARK

KALEPOLEPO PARK
Menehune Shores
Koa Lagoon

1

Kihei Gateway Center
gas

Pi'ikea St.

Waipu'ilani

6

KIHEI

Maui Sunset

WAIOHULI BEACH

Ulunui

Long's
Center

Azeka Center I
Star Market
gas

Azeka II

E. Lipoa St.

Maui Gardens

S. Kihei

golf
course

7

KALAMA BEACH PARK

P

E. Welakahao Rd.
Kukui Mall
Kihei Town Center
Foodland

library

Ahuana

COVE PARK

Kanani

Kalama Village
Shores of Maui

CHARLEY YOUNG BEACH

KAMA'OLE I

Royal Mauian

gas

ABC Plaza
Dolphin Plaza
Rainbow Mall
Kama'ole Center

KAMA'OLE II

Ke Ali'i Alanui

Keonekai

KAMA'OLE III

Kama'ole
Sands

Pi'ilani Hwy.

N

KIHEI PUBLIC BOAT RAMP

Mana Kai Maui
Hale Hui Kai

P

Kilohana Dr.

Mapu St.

P

Maui
Meadows

KEAWAKAPU BEACH

Okolani Dr.

to Wailea

(31)

Cove Park

This tiny park is tucked in a corner between Kalama Beach Park and and Kama'ole I Beach Park. It offers a bit of sand and a very pretty view, but parking isn't easy. There's a bit of snorkeling too, but not really much to see.

GETTING THERE   Driving north on S. Kihei Rd., continue past Kalama Park and Shores of Maui, then watch carefully or you'll miss it (see map, page 77).

Charley Young Beach Park

This pretty little spot offers a sandy beach, no crowds and even has a shower. Parking, however, isn't great – with just three spaces. It's a nice place for a swim and a shower. Snorkeling is possible, but there generally isn't much to see near shore.

GETTING THERE   Between Cove Park and Kam I, this beach is hidden at the end of Kai'au Place (off S. Kihei Rd.). If you take this road toward the ocean, you'll see the little blue beach access sign (see map, page 77).

Kama'ole I, II & III Beach Parks

These three beach are all in a row on the makai side of S. Kihei Rd. They offer sandy beaches, lovely views and good swimming most of the year. You can walk the full length of all three by climbing up and over the small rocky points that separate them. They are popular spots for sunning, swimming, playing and enjoying the sunset. Snorkeling here is possible when calm, but there really isn't much to see. These parks do provide good sites to learn how to snorkel and you'll see a bit of coral with some very pretty fish.

GETTING THERE   Kam I, II and III are well-marked along S. Kihei Rd. south of the center of Kihei. All offer some parking, grass, shade, soft sandy beaches and restrooms. The beaches are usually relatively calm. Waves can pick up along this section of Maui when there is south swell (usually in the summer), so head elsewhere on the island if this happens. Afternoons can be a bit choppy too, so try to snorkel or swim before noon for the calmest conditions.

Kihei Boat Ramp

Since the public boat ramp provides a small breakwater and has a sandy beach to one side (to the north), this is an easy entry point for snorkeling in the south Kihei area. The snorkeling here is good if calm enough to head straight out where the water is about 10-20 feet deep. You do have to watch out for boats entering the ramp area. This is another good spot to watch for turtles – especially in the deeper areas.

GETTING THERE   From Kihei, take South Kihei Road until you see the boat ramp on the ocean side of the road. You'll find a parking lot with plenty of space, grassy area with trees, picnic tables as well as restrooms and a shower.

Doctor My Eyes

If you are swimming along snorkeling peacefully and your vision suddenly loses focus, don't be too quick to panic and call for a doctor. While you may have had a stroke or the water may be oily, there is a much more likely cause: You've probably just entered into an outdoor demonstration of the refractive qualities of mixtures of clear liquids of different densities. Is that perfectly clear?

Near the edge of some protected bays, clear spring water oozes smoothly out into the saltwater. As it is lighter than the mineral-laden saltwater, it tends to float in a layer near the surface for a time.

Now, clear spring water is easy to see through, as is clear saltwater. If you mix them thoroughly, you have dilute saltwater, still clear. But when the two float side by side, the light going through them is bent and re-bent as it passes between them, and this blurs your vision. It's much like the blurring produced when hot, lighter air rises off black pavement, and produces wavy vision and mirage.

These lenses of clear water drift about, and often disappear as quickly as they appeared. Swimming away from the source of the spring water usually solves the problem. Clear at last?

Keawakapu Beach Park

This long, skinny park stretches along a mile of sandy beach just south of Kihei. There are three public accesses (#108, #109 and #110) and two parking lots, although all are easy to miss (see map, page 192). The central access offers better parking and a shower, but no other facilities. This is a nice spot for families to enjoy the sand, calm water and lovely view. Snorkeling is best from the south access where you can snorkel toward the left. The water in front of the beach park is all rather shallow with a fair amount of rocks and mediocre snorkeling. No restrooms are available.

GETTING THERE   From Kihei, take South Kihei Road. This road will dead-end at the southern access to the park. See map, page 81 for more information about the three public accesses and parking.

Heading south on Highway 31, turn right on Kilohana Drive, which will take you directly to a parking lot for Keawakapu Beach at the corner of South Kihei Road.

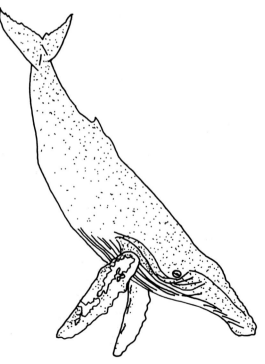

humpback whale

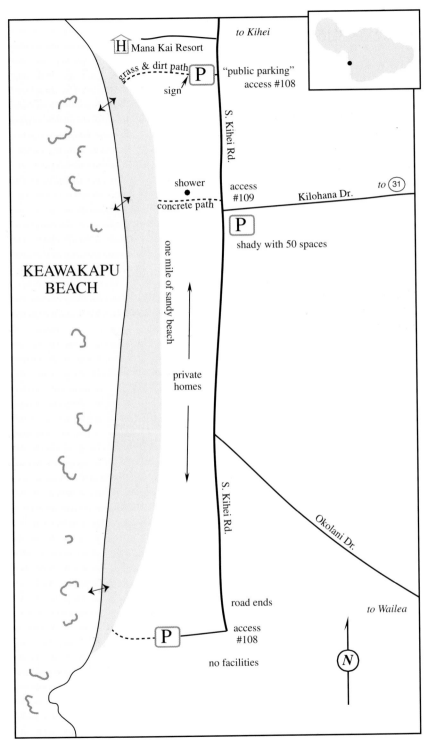

H Mana Kai Resort

to Kihei

grass & dirt path

P "public parking" access #108

sign

S. Kihei Rd.

shower

concrete path

access #109

Kilohana Dr.

to 31

P

shady with 50 spaces

KEAWAKAPU BEACH

one mile of sandy beach

private homes

S. Kihei Rd.

Okolani Dr.

road ends

to Wailea

N

access #108

P

no facilities

81

Wailea Area

The western coast of South Maui has been growing rapidly in recent years. This is a beautiful area located beneath the rain shadow of Haleakala with views of several islands off the coast. Huge hotels of various styles have been built on terrific beaches. Other equally nice beaches remain secluded for the time being.

There are relatively few condos here (but some are excellent) and prices are usually high. Hotel styles and sizes vary, so select a hotel to your taste or choose a good beach and settle for what accommodations are there. This is really a great place for snorkelers, from beginners to advanced. It's not quite as calm as the little bays in West Maui, but it has plenty of coves, points, pretty beaches and lava fields.

With reef extending far out to sea, Wailea hosts lots of turtles and interesting fish. All in all, an excellent location for serious snorkelers. If the prices are too steep for your pocketbook, stay in the Kihei area and drive here to snorkel.

Wailea is becoming more and more popular, so highway 31 will probably gradually be extended as the land is developed.

The beaches of Wailea offer broad soft sand, calm snorkeling, and gorgeous views of nearby islands. On a clear day you can see West Maui, Lana'i, Kaho'olawe, Pu'u 'Ola'i (Red Hill), and Molokini. We've snorkeled the whole Wailea coast from Keawakapu Beach Park to Polo Beach. Snorkeling is best here before noon, when the cool breezes arrive making the water choppy – sometimes even dangerous. With chop snorkels, we don't mind the wind-driven choppy conditions as long as the waves and currents don't pick up too much. Beginners are likely to prefer mornings – the earlier, the better.

Hawai'ian turkeyfish

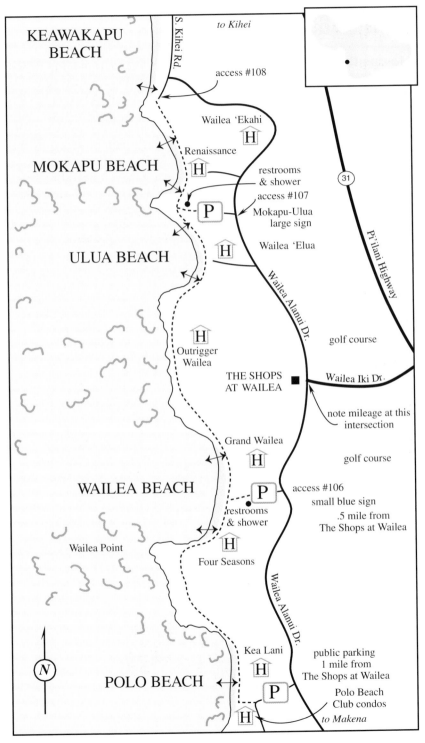

KEAWAKAPU
BEACH

to Kihei

S. Kihei Rd.

access #108

Wailea 'Ekahi

H

Renaissance

MOKAPU BEACH

H

restrooms
& shower

access #107

Mokapu-Ulua
large sign

P

Wailea 'Elua

H

ULUA BEACH

31

Pi'ilani Highway

Wailea Alanui Dr.

golf course

H

Outrigger
Wailea

THE SHOPS
AT WAILEA

Wailea Iki Dr.

note mileage at this
intersection

golf course

Grand Wailea

H

WAILEA BEACH

P

access #106

small blue sign

.5 mile from
The Shops at Wailea

restrooms
& shower

Wailea Point

H

Four Seasons

Wailea Alanui Dr.

N

Kea Lani

H

public parking
1 mile from
The Shops at Wailea

POLO BEACH

P

Polo Beach
Club condos

H

to Makena

83

Mokapu Beach

Mokapu Beach is where you end up if you snorkel from Ulua Beach north completely around the point. Just to be different, you can begin your snorkel here and end up at Ulua – assuming you plan to snorkel the whole point. It would be too far for most beginners, but is quite easy for an intermediate snorkeler. This makes an excellent one-way snorkel if you walk back on the beach path provided by the hotels. Mornings are the calmest time for snorkeling out past the point. The coral and numbers of fish increase as you head out to deeper water (about 15 feet deep). While you'll find coral and fish near shore, you won't find large numbers.

GETTING THERE   Take Highway 31 south past Kihei and turn right on Wailea Iki Drive at the end of the highway (see map, page 192). At the end of Wailea Iki Drive, turn right on Wailea Alanui Drive and watch for the big sign that says Mokapu-Ulua Beach (access #107). You'll find parking, showers, restrooms, picnic tables, a grassy hill and shade. Come early if you want a parking spot near the beach. Mokapu is the beach just to the north of this beautiful point. So Mokapu is on your right, while Ulua is in front. This stretch of beaches in front of the big hotels all connects by a walkway.

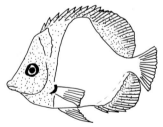

pyramid butterflyfish

84

Ulua Beach Park

At this very popular snorkeling and shore diving spot, you can snorkel around the point to the right or far out to sea as well. Coral and fish are plentiful. This beach is best snorkeled before the noon winds arrive. Picnic on the grassy hill at the north end of the beach and enjoy the gorgeous view. All amenities are available.

This is a very popular spot, so come early or late if you want to avoid crowds (before 9:00 a.m. or after 3:00 p.m.). Experienced snorkelers can easily swim beyond the crowd of beginners who tend to stay close to shore. This is an excellent site, with lots to see, a beautiful setting, and a reasonable amount of parking. When calm, it's easy to snorkel around the point to Mokapu Beach. In fact, a good swimmer can snorkel all the way to Keawakapu Beach Park. A beach walkway connects all these beaches, making a one-way snorkel simple.

Most of the water is only about ten feet deep with scattered patches of reef that extend well beyond the point. You're likely to see some of the green sea turtles in this area as well as schools of reef fish. Large numbers of turtles hang out on the reef further from shore – especially where the reef drops down to twenty feet deep.

GETTING THERE   Ulua is the beach in front of the Stouffer Wailea Beach Resort, with lots of big resorts nearby (see map, page 83). Take Highway 31 south past Kihei and watch for Wailea Iki Drive to the right heading toward the resorts. At The Shops at Wailea turn right on Wailea Alanui Road toward the Stouffer Wailea Beach Resort. You'll quickly see a large sign for Mokapu-Ulua Beach. This is public access #107. Drop people and gear at the beach near the showers and restrooms, then send the driver off to locate a parking spot. As Ulua becomes ever more popular, you will need to arrive early in the morning for space, but that's the best time to snorkel here anyway.

Wailea Beach

Snorkeling is best at the south end of the beach toward the point. Early in the day it's usually calmer, while the wind typically picks up by noon making for choppy conditions. When calm, this beach offers good snorkeling as you head out to sea. You're almost sure to see turtles if you stay in the water for awhile. Please remember they are protected by Hawai'ian law, so don't touch them, hover over them or chase them.

The reef here extends about a mile toward the sea and is shallow enough for snorkeling most of the way out. Stay closer to shore if it gets choppy or you encounter any current. On a calm day we saw many turtles, a snowflake eel, numerous large tangs, needlefish, red pencil urchins as well as the usual reef dwellers.

The public access offers parking, restrooms and showers.

GETTING THERE   This beach is between the Grand Hyatt Wailea Resort to the south, and the Four Seasons Hotel to the north (see map, page 192). From Highway 31, turn right on Wailea Iki Drive, then left on Wailea Alanui Road at The Shops at Wailea to the first public access (access #106). Watch carefully for a small blue public access sign (easy to miss!) and turn right between the Grand Wailea and the Four Seasons hotels. Here you'll find a parking lot for about 50 cars, then another for about 20, followed by restrooms and showers. Take the path directly to the beach. From the sand, snorkel to the left towards the point and around if calm enough.

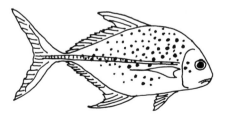

bluefin trevally jack

Polo Beach

Not the best snorkeling or swimming in Wailea, but it's OK and you'll find public access, adequate parking and good facilities. This is also a pleasant spot for a picnic. Polo Beach is located between the huge white turrets of Kea Lani Hotel (which can't be missed, even if you close your eyes) and the tall Polo Beach condo building. The main drawback of this picturesque beach is that's it's a little rocky with less clearance than the beaches to the north. Strong swimmers can snorkel from here to Ulua or Wailea. The beach walkway will bring you back to Polo Beach. Since the beach here is a little more shallow than the rest of Wailea, you will probably prefer high tide for an easier entrance. The park has a path to the beach, restrooms, shower, picnic tables and a lovely view.

GETTING THERE   From Highway 31, take a right toward Wailea, then a left on Wailea Alanui Road when you must turn (see map, page 83). From this corner, continue one mile south on Wailea Alanui Road to the public access for Polo Beach parking.

Chang's Beach (Makena Surf)

Chang's Beach at the Makena Surf condos is an easily-missed, but delightful, beach with excellent safe swimming and snorkeling. The beach is entirely surrounded by the two-story Makena Surf condos, but good public access is provided, if you look carefully. No public facilities are available except a shower.

This beach is really a small, perfect gem in every way and is one of our Maui favorites. It combines a pretty and serene beach, hard to beat easy access from sand for swimming and good snorkeling in a calm bay When south swell arrive, this beach is calmer than most in the area because the sand slopes so gently providing easier waves.

As usual in Maui on an exposed beach, waves can pick up after noon, so come early to avoid choppy water. The large, deluxe condos are available for rent, and make a great family base if the rental rates don't send you into shock.

GETTING THERE   Go south on Highway 31, turning right toward Wailea on Wailea Iki Drive, then left on Wailea Alanui Road when you come to the big shopping center and have to turn one way or the other (see map, page 89). Turn left and continue south for 3.5 miles from this intersection. Watch for the rock walls surrounding the Makena Surf. There is a small entrance to a nine-car public parking lot with a little blue "public access #104" sign posted in an inconspicuous spot.

The paved, shady trail starts at the front left of the parking lot where you will go through a gate (see map, page 89). Just follow the winding trail downhill through the flowers to the beach. Snorkel the left side of the beach, just steps from the end of the path.

Finding your way back up to your car can be the hardest part. It's all too seasy to wander off on one of the side trails that dead-end at sections of the condos. From the beach, the trail leads straight to a Y. Be sure to angle right here. Go left at the next Y and you'll find the shower on your right. Check our map first. If you end up in the wrong parking lot, you won't even be able to get out to the street due to the gates, so you'll have to double back almost to the beach.

88

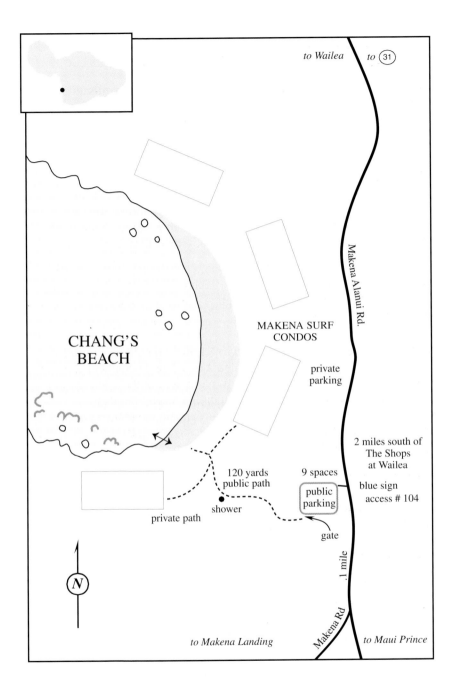

to Wailea   to (31)

Makena Alanui Rd.

MAKENA SURF
CONDOS

CHANG'S
BEACH

private
parking

2 miles south of
The Shops
at Wailea

120 yards
public path

9 spaces

blue sign
access # 104

public
parking

shower

private path

gate

N

.1 mile

to Makena Landing

Makena Rd

to Maui Prince

89

Five Graves/Caves

This popular area includes several entries ranging in difficulty from beginner to advanced and is often snorkeled by boat access. There are plenty of turtles in the area as well as interesting canyons and coves. It's often a better site for Scuba than for snorkeling when conditions are a little rougher. It has a tendency to be choppy as well as murky.

Still, on a nice day it can make for very enjoyable snorkeling, especially when the visibility is good enough to see the turtles. They often rest on the bottom, which is fifteen to twenty feet deep here. Look sharp in sandy pockets among the coral and you'll be rewarded.

GETTING THERE   Go south on Highway 31, turning right toward Wailea on Wailea Iki Drive, then left at The Shops at Wailea on Wailea Alanui Road (see map, page 192). Watch for Makena Road to your right just past the Makena Surf condos. Just two tenths of a mile from the turnoff to Makena Road, you'll reach the Five Graves area (see map, page 91). There is a tiny parking area on the beach side of the road (about ten cars) and a short path heads towards the water, passing the graves. This path angles toward a narrow cove where divers often enter. Entering from this cove is definitely not for beginners because the rocks are slippery and the surf unpredictable here. However, it does place you right in the middle of the best snorkeling.

Makena Landing

For easier street access to Five Graves/Caves, but a longer swim, continue on Makena Road to the Makena Landing County Park (access #103), where you'll find a parking lot on the right with a shower and restrooms on the left near the sand (see map, page 192).

Entry is best at the right side in the corner near the parking lot. There is a small, sandy beach offering easy access. Snorkel to the right and around the point as far as seems calm.

Another entry point is over rock from the middle of the parking lot. It's a bit trickier, but handy if the water's calm enough and you're careful to avoid slipping on the rocks. This gets you out closer to the point where you'll find the best snorkeling. There is also a neat little entry cove just ten feet beyond the parking lot, but it's marked "private property."

90

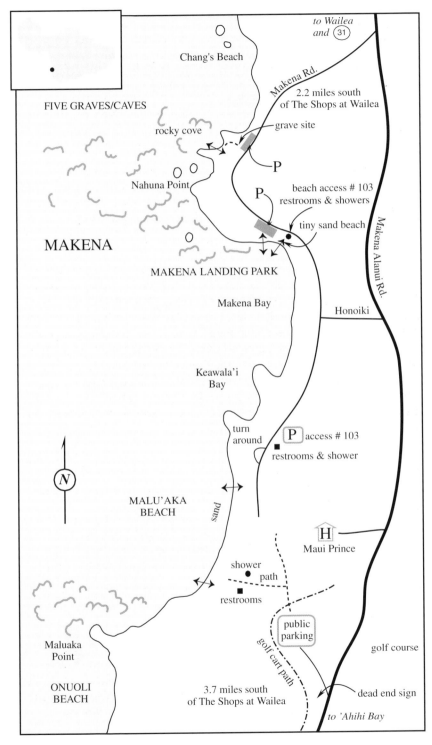

FIVE GRAVES/CAVES

to Wailea
and ③¹

Chang's Beach

Makena Rd.

2.2 miles south
of The Shops at Wailea

rocky cove

grave site

P

Nahuna Point

P

beach access # 103
restrooms & showers

tiny sand beach

MAKENA

MAKENA LANDING PARK

Makena Bay

Makena Alanui Rd.

Honoiki

Keawala'i
Bay

turn
around

P access # 103
restrooms & shower

N

MALU'AKA
BEACH

sand

H
Maui Prince

shower
path

restrooms

public
parking

golf course

Maluaka
Point

golf cart path

dead end sign

ONUOLI
BEACH

3.7 miles south
of The Shops at Wailea

to 'Ahihi Bay

91

GETTING THERE   Go south on Highway 31, turning right toward Wailea on Wailea Iki Drive, then left on Wailea Alanui Road (see map, page 91). Watch for Makena Road to your right just past the Makena Surf condos. Continue on Makena Road until you see the Makena Landing County Park where you will see a parking lot with shower on the right and restrooms near the sand on the left.

juvenile yellowtail coris

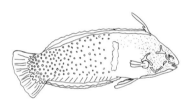

adult yellowtail coris

juvenile rockmover wrasse

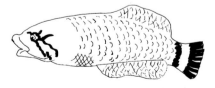

adult rockmover wrasse

Malu'aka Beach

Malu'aka Beach in front of the Maui Prince Hotel is an excellent all-around site. The south end of this lovely beach offers wonderful snorkeling and easy entry from the sand. It is serene, relatively uncrowded, and home to a large number of turtles. We have seen some Picasso triggerfish right near shore. This beautiful and relatively uncommon fish appears to be painted with water colors.

At the far south end of the beach a grassy hill has gorgeous views, picnic tables, shade, restrooms and showers. A delightful swimming, snorkeling or picnic spot. The view includes Molokini, Lana'i, Kaho'olawe, Pu'u 'Ola'i (Red Hill) and West Maui in the distance.

Malu'aka also tends to be fairly calm (especially before noon), so can be great for beginning snorkelers. The further out you swim, the more turtles you're likely to see. This is where we saw the largest turtle we've encountered in Maui. Mornings are best, since the swells can pick up around noon. This is one of Maui's prettiest spots and remains surprisingly uncrowded. We highly recommend this beach as well as the understated graceful Maui Prince Hotel.

GETTING THERE   Going south on Highway 31, turn right toward Wailea on Wailea Iki Drive (see map, page 91). Highway 31 dead ends here. At The Shops at Wailea turn left on Wailea Alanui Road. Note your mileage at this point. In 3.6 miles you'll see a small road on your right that doubles back and has a sign that says "dead end". This road is very easy to miss if you forget to note the mileage (see map, page 83). There is a golf path on the far side of the little road, so you'll know it's the right one. Take this a short few blocks to the small parking lot holding about twenty cars. There's an easy path to the beach – about 100 yards. You'll see restrooms and picnic tables on your left. To the right is a shower.

Snorkel along the reef on the left, which is quite extensive. In calm weather, you can snorkel directly over the reef with plenty of clearance for an excellent close-up view of the coral and fish. In calm weather with bright sun, this reef is delightful. Snorkel only outside the reef's edge when swells get higher.

An alternative access to this beach is from Makena Road leading to the north end of the beach. You'll find a public parking lot on the left side of the road with restrooms and shower about 200 yards before you get to the north end of the beach. Passengers can be dropped off much closer. From this end of the beach you can snorkel to the right or hike across the beach and snorkel the southern side of Malu'aka.

Onuoli Beach (Black Sand Beach)

This beach is uncrowded, compared with the rest of Makena State Park because it doesn't offer good swimming or surfing. The beach is quite shallow making it more challenging at low tide. Snorkeling is good, but not spectacular in the shallow areas near shore. If you don't see turtles, just continue out to the deeper water (about twenty feet deep). When seas are calm, a strong swimmer can snorkel all the way around the red cliffs to Pu'u 'Ola'i with ease. This site offers protection from summer south swells that hit Big Beach quite hard.

Black Sand Beach is better for snorkeling than swimming since the whole beach contains coral underfoot. There aren't terrific numbers of fish. Still, there's a good variety of some of the prettiest fish with turtles almost a sure sighting. No facilities are available here – other than a parking lot right near the shore. When waves do arrive at Black Sand Beach, it's best to snorkel elsewhere because you don't want to get caught between coral and waves.

GETTING THERE   Going south on Highway 31, take Wailea Iki to the right until you see The Shops at Wailea. Here, take Wailea Alanui Rd. south (noting the mileage at this corner). At 3.9 miles from this corner you'll see a dirt road toward Red Hill (see map, page 95). This .3-mile road winds back to Black Sand Beach (really sort of gray), where you can park near the sea. When very calm and not during the lowest tides, this is a good site for beginners. More experienced snorkelers will enjoy heading around the hill to the left (south) as far as Pu'u 'Ola'i Beach.

Pu'u 'Ola'i (Little Beach)

Pu'u 'Ola'i is also called Little Beach. From the parking lot at Oneloa, also called Big Beach, where the sign says "Makena State Park", walk straight down the shady, flat path to the long, sandy beach with some facilities (picnic tables, portable toilets, no shower) and a lifeguard at times.

This is a very popular swimming and sunbathing spot with plenty of sand and some shade. Just beyond the lifeguard station at the far right is a path leading up the hill to Pu'u 'Ola'i, which is a traditional nude beach. It also happens to be an excellent snorkeling spot when calm.

From the beach at Pu'i 'Ola'i, snorkel to the right as far as it is calm enough – or even straight out to sea. There are lots of little canyons,

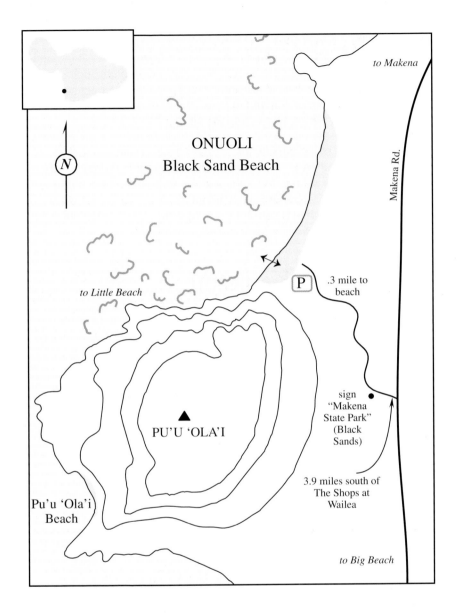

to Makena

ONUOLI
Black Sand Beach

Makena Rd.

N

to Little Beach

P   .3 mile to beach

▲
PU'U 'OLA'I

sign
"Makena
State Park"
(Black
Sands)

3.9 miles south of
The Shops at
Wailea

Pu'u 'Ola'i
Beach

to Big Beach

coves, good coral, large and numerous turtles, and plenty of fish variety (although not huge numbers of fish). The snorkeling is definitely worth the hike. When calm, you can snorkel all the way around either point, with good snorkeling the entire way.

Note: To avoid confusion, remember there are other Makena and Oneloa beaches on Maui, thus the popularity of the names Big and Little. Onuoli Beach to the north of Pu'u 'Ola'i is also called Black Sand Beach and also has a sign that says Makena State Park.

GETTING THERE   Going south on Highway 31, turn right on Wailea Iki Drive toward The Shops at Wailea, then left on Wailea Alanui Road and continue south. The Big Beach turnoff is 4 miles south of this point (see map, page 97). This is the old parking lot, but provides the best access to the north end of the beach and to Little Beach. A new and larger lot has been built two tenths of a mile to the south.

At the beach side of the parking lot is a path marked with a sign that says "Makena State Park". Follow the path 180 yards to the beach, then continue across the sand to the right past the lifeguard station until you see a narrow path over the small hill (about fifty feet high). Walk 240 yards to Pu'u 'Ola'i (Little Beach). It's a fairly easy path, but not flat, and requires some minor climbing over the edge of the hill.

Oneloa Beach (Big Beach)

This popular beach, usually referred to as Big Beach, is best for swimming, sunning, picnics and socializing. It often has a fair surf, and is popular for body surfing and boogie boarding. At times (especially with southern swell), it can be too rough for safety.

Snorkeling is best around the point between Big and Little Beaches, and is possible only when conditions are calm enough. It is often possible to snorkel all the way to Pu'u 'Ola'i from the northern end near the lifeguard station at Big Beach. Mornings are always better here for snorkelers because the waves usually pick up in the afternoon.

If you want to snorkel, be sure to park in the lot at the far north since this is indeed one BIG Beach. You'll find plenty of wide sandy beach, picnic tables, portable toilets, but no showers. Beginners will find the hike to Pu'u 'Ola'i much easier than the long snorkel even on a calm day. Good swimmers (preferably with wetsuits) can snorkel all the way from Big Beach to Black Sand Beach.

GETTING THERE   Going south on Highway 31, turn right on Wailea Iki Drive. At The Shops at Wailea, note the mileage, turn left on Wailea Alanui Road and continue south for four miles. This is the old parking lot and is the one closest to the snorkeling. There is a larger parking lot at the next exit to the south. On the beach side of the parking lot, you will see a wide path marked "Makena State Park" and it takes you down a shady path directly to the beach, about 180 yards (see map, page 97).

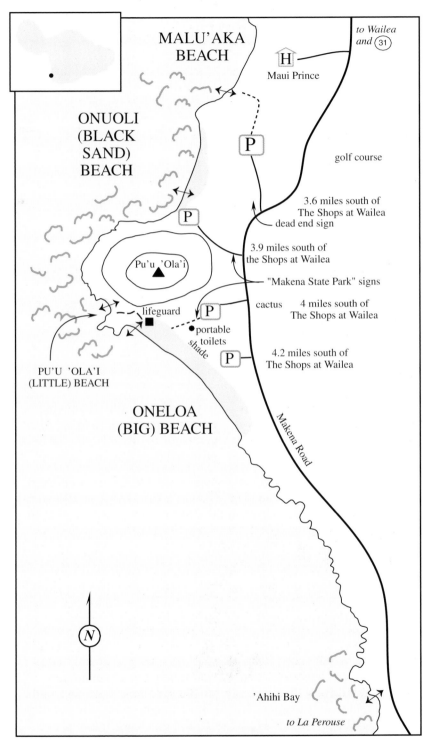

MALU'AKA BEACH

ONUOLI (BLACK SAND) BEACH

Pu'u 'Ola'i

lifeguard

PU'U 'OLA'I (LITTLE) BEACH

ONELOA (BIG) BEACH

H Maui Prince

to Wailea and (31)

golf course

P

P

3.6 miles south of The Shops at Wailea dead end sign

3.9 miles south of the Shops at Wailea

"Makena State Park" signs

cactus   4 miles south of The Shops at Wailea

P

portable toilets

shade

P   4.2 miles south of The Shops at Wailea

Makena Road

N

'Ahihi Bay

to La Perouse

97

Kanahena Hidden Beach

This beautiful hidden beach offers a pleasant, unusual picnic spot (particularly in the summer or fall) after you snorkel 'Ahihi Cove, which has no sand. It's completely hidden from view, although right next to Makena Road, sandwiched between two stylish oceanfront homes. The sand at this tiny beach is powdery soft and white – with more sand in the summer. Ringed by palms, bougainvillaea, high stone walls and a view of Molokini and Kahalo'owe, it offers a secluded spot to relax, wade, and enjoy the beauty. If you try it, you may have the beach to yourselves! Modest snorkeling is possible, but only when there is little or no swell, due to lots of sharp a'a rocks. No facilities.

GETTING THERE   Going south on Makena Rd., about half a mile south of Big Beach, watch for a high stone wall on the ocean side of the road. There is a narrow gap in the wall for beach access just south of house #6900. Across the street (mauka) you will see house #6925 with a chain link fence. Take the narrow twenty-foot path to the sand.

'Ahihi Cove

One of our Maui favorites, this gem is a beautiful tiny cove with fairly clear water and lots to see – even a large eel close to shore to awe the little kids. Entry is a bit slippery from the old concrete boat ramp at the far right, so sit down and work your way in carefully.

The cove itself is quite calm and shallow (five to fifteen feet deep) and the reef extends far out. This bay has a wonderful variety within a small space, so it is well worth the drive even if you're staying in the north. Another must see!

Beginners can have a great time close to shore where there are plenty of large and varied fish. More advanced snorkelers can venture out beyond into the larger bay. This is actually a tiny cove within a large, protected area. It has too much coral and rock to be a good swimming spot. Snorkel any direction. It's all fascinating snorkeling, but has no facilities and only a tiny, rocky beach.

We have seen huge parrotfish, all sorts of butterflyfish and tangs, Moorish idols, triggerfish, wrasses and much more, like a large aquarium, but from the inside. Out further to the left we have seen octopus and beautiful coral. If it's calm enough, swim way out to the left. The right side is good too. Don't miss this bay! Beginners

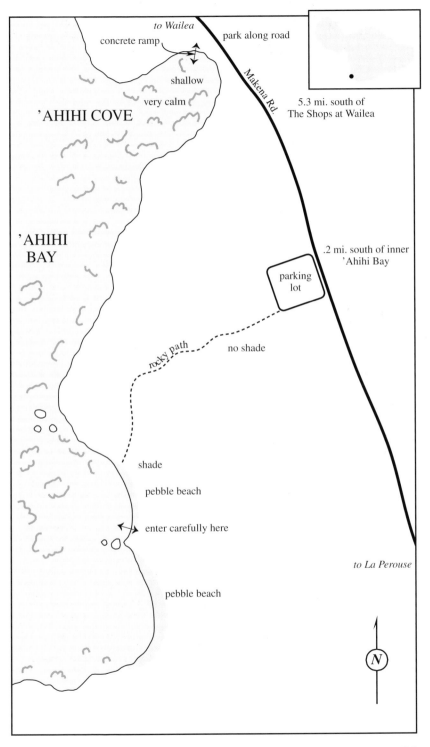

to Wailea

concrete ramp

park along road

Makena Rd.

5.3 mi. south of
The Shops at Wailea

shallow

very calm

'AHIHI COVE

'AHIHI
BAY

.2 mi. south of inner
'Ahihi Bay

parking
lot

rocky path

no shade

shade

pebble beach

enter carefully here

to La Perouse

pebble beach

N

99

should practice elsewhere first to be competent enough to avoid kicking the fragile reef. There are no sandy areas for beginners to stop and stand. Entry can be tricky if south swell is high, since the entry area is shallow.

GETTING THERE   Going south on Highway 31, take the Wailea Iki Drive turnoff to the right toward the hotels (see map, page 83). Then at The Shops at Wailea, turn left on Wailea Alanui Road. Note the mileage at this intersection in order to determine the location of several of these beaches. 'Ahihi Cove is 5.3 miles south of this intersection. The road will continue south eventually crossing bare lava, narrow but still an adequate road.

First you'll see walls surrounding some lovely (and expensive) homes. Then at 'Ahihi Cove, you'll see the cove on your right as the road narrows to one lane and curves left, skirting the tiny cove. You'll also see some houses and trees here (see map, page 99). Park along the road wherever there is space. If parking happens to fill, there is a dirt parking lot just two tenths of a mile further south.

Enter the water on the far right (north) corner of the cove, only ten feet from the road. The old concrete ramp provides a little slide into the water. The beach itself is rocky rather than sandy and quite small. Just so you're sure this is the right place – you'll see stone walls and a telephone pole marked T5 just before the cove. Avoid when waves hit the shore because this inner cove is all fairly shallow and filled with sharp coral.

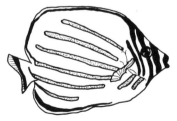

ornate butterflyfish

'Ahihi Bay

You'll find a parking lot just beyond 'Ahihi Cove. This is an extensive and excellent spot for experienced snorkelers. It's not really suited to beginners (unless it's unusually calm) or swimmers since entry can be a bit difficult and there are plenty of rocks.

There's plenty of space in the dirt parking lot. You must hike down a somewhat rocky path with little shade until you reach the beach. Shoes are a must here.

Snorkeling is uncrowded and excellent with great views of Haleakala in the background and Molokini Island out to sea. Be sure to lift your head out of the water now and then to enjoy the fabulous views towards shore. You'll want to try this one more than once because it offers such a large area to explore.

We have seen turtles, eels, colorful coral, schools of raccoon butterflyfish, scrawled filefish, bird wrasses, sailfin tangs, frogfish and a huge school of Heller's barracuda (just after entering the water). Come early in the day for the calmest conditions. You'll want to snorkel for a long time, so wear a wetsuit if you have one. We highly recommend this whole snorkeling area if you are somewhat experienced and conditions are calm.

GETTING THERE   Go two tenths of a mile past 'Ahihi Cove and turn right, parking in this open area (see map, page 99). The path starts straight toward the water and angles to the left until it reaches the rocky beach (about 200 yards of relatively easy path – compared to the a'a lava on both sides). At the beach, continue another 100 yards south (to your left) across the gravel beach to just before the next little point where entry is easier over a bit of sand.

There's a nice shady spot to leave your stuff and you'll find the entry easier than it appears from a distance. Once out in the bay, snorkel to the right near shore as well as further out to see the variety. Our favorite spot is off the point about halfway to 'Ahihi Cove. Getting out is quite easy but you should make sure to return to the same spot. If you'd like a one-way snorkel, swim all the way into 'Ahihi Cove and take the short hike back to your car. Of course, this one-way snorkel works best if you wear booties or carry plastic shoes along as you snorkel. We highly recommend this snorkeling area if you are somewhat experienced and conditions are calm.

Fish Pond

This trail through 'Ahihi-Kina'u is VERY difficult to spot (in fact, you won't believe it's a trail across the a'a) and requires a half-hour hike across the bare black lava field. However, it leads to good snorkeling and picnicking at a beautiful, secluded cove (a natural little harbor). A small peninsula protects this cove from most waves, so it is unusually calm and clear. This is a charming fine-sand beach where you can enjoy a good snorkel, then a quiet bag lunch. You may have the bay to yourselves although kayakers sometimes stop here.

It is definitely worth the hike, but you must wear sturdy closed-toe shoes to protect your feet from the sharp black lava. Bring sunglasses, water and a hat too, since the trail is completely exposed and the black lava really holds the heat in the summer. Of course, no facilities of any sort are available here. This is a great spot to enjoy the early evening, but take care to allow enough time to hike out before dark because this sharp lava trail would really be challenging without a light.

GETTING THERE   Driving south on Highway 31, turn right on Wailea Iki Drive toward The Shops at Wailea (see map, page 83). Note your mileage at the shops, head left on Wailea Alanui Road. Continue past 'Ahihi Bay, which is 5.3 miles from this corner. Less than a mile past the bay, you'll see telephone pole #17. Watch for the next telephone pole, which should be #18, but isn't marked (see map, page 103). The unmarked trail to the water starts twenty yards north of this pole. Parking is available at small turnouts about 150 yards in either direction.

You'll be able to recognize the trail by a few small splashes of white paint on a water pipe along the edge of the road. The first part of the trail definitely doesn't look promising, but gets easier soon. You'll know you're on the trail when you see the sign "'Ahihi-Kina'i Reserve" about twenty yards in from the road. Follow this trail very carefully all the way to the water, where entry is quite easy from a pebble beach. Watch the trail as you go to ensure you won't get lost on your return. The trail itself makes for an interesting hike. Watch for scattered ferns and small trees struggling to survive on this dramatic, but barren, landscape.

There is a connecting trail of sorts leading south to the next trail we mention. However, it is not well marked and is very difficult to follow. You could wind up hiking cross-country across rugged a'a lava, which we definitely don't recommend.

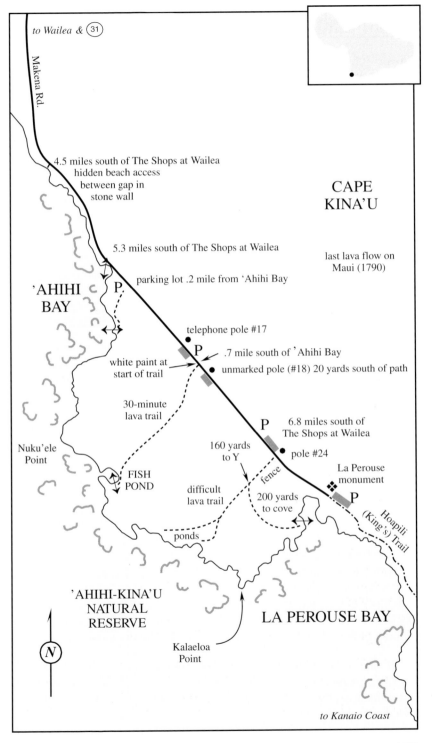

to Wailea & (31)

Makena Rd.

4.5 miles south of The Shops at Wailea
hidden beach access
between gap in
stone wall

5.3 miles south of The Shops at Wailea

parking lot .2 mile from 'Ahihi Bay

'AHIHI
BAY

P

CAPE
KINA'U

last lava flow on
Maui (1790)

telephone pole #17

P

.7 mile south of 'Ahihi Bay

white paint at
start of trail

unmarked pole (#18) 20 yards south of path

30-minute
lava trail

P

6.8 miles south of
The Shops at Wailea

pole #24

Nuku'ele
Point

160 yards
to Y

fence

La Perouse
monument

P

FISH
POND

difficult
lava trail

200 yards
to cove

Hoapili
(King's) Trail

ponds

'AHIHI-KINA'U
NATURAL
RESERVE

LA PEROUSE BAY

N

Kalaeloa
Point

to Kanaio Coast

103

'Ahihi-Kina'u Reserve

'Ahihi-Kina'u Natural Area Reserve is quite a large area, with one marked path that leads to a snorkeling site. It's another excellent spot, secluded, with room to explore, although you must hike over a sharp lava path to reach it. Reef shoes or tennis shoes are absolutely necessary on this path. It's a bare and rugged, but beautiful, 360-yard hike – not at all steep. Watch the trail carefully because you don't want to wander out onto the a'a lava.

Entry is from smooth lava rock at the end of the trail, but it's not difficult if you take it slow and careful. This is usually a very calm, well-protected spot. When waves kick up at other beaches, it can be murky here in spite of looking perfectly calm. The water tends to be more clear as you head out a bit.

Leave something like a brightly-colored bag where you enter, so you can snorkel your way back to the right place. You'll definitely require the path to get back to your car. For snorkeling, wander in any direction as long as you stay within the calm protected area.

This site has plenty of variety of fish, turtles, eels, etc., but the coral isn't spectacular. The Reserve tends to be murky (a milky look), so we had to snorkel out beyond the small cove before we could see much.

GETTING THERE   Driving south on Highway 31, turn right on Wailea Iki Dr. toward The Shops at Wailea (see map, page 83). Then turn left on Wailea Alanui Road, and be sure to note your mileage at this intersection. Continue south even after the road heads across the bare lava. Pass the little 'Ahihi Bay at 5.3 miles. At 6.8 miles from the shops you'll see the 'Ahihi-Kina'u sign (see map, page 103). Park along the road. The telephone pole at the trail is #24.

Take the trail toward the water with a fence to your left for about about 160 yards over rough lava. Wear close-toed shoes and stay on the trail. This is hardly the place for impromptu shortcuts. At about 160 yards, take the Y to your left and hike another 200 yards. This trail will eventually end at the little cove where you can enter safely (just watch out for slippery rocks). You'll probably have the entire bay to yourselves.

Watch your entry point carefully, because you will want to come out at the same place in order to end up back on the trail. Wear a hat and bring water because there's little shade and no facilities. This trail over black lava can be very hot in the summer.

The trail continues to the right where you took the Y to the left. Although the trail continues to the ocean and a couple of unusual ponds, it is very rough and difficult, and not a snorkeling destination.

La Perouse Bay

When the English explorer Captain James Cook made the first European contact with Hawai'i in 1778, he described and mapped a large bay stretching from the great cinder cone Pu'u 'Ola'i in the north, to Cape Hanamanoia in the south. Called 'Ahihi Bay, it had a magnificent long sandy beach.

Another English sailor, George Vancouver, called on Maui in 1792 (Maui was already becoming a popular vacation destination.) But what Vancouver saw at 'Ahihi Bay must have astounded him. For in 1790, the last great lava flow on Maui had formed Cape Kina'u, projecting more than a mile out and two miles wide right in the middle of 'Ahihi Bay! Now there were two bays, 'Ahihi and one further south now known as La Perouse Bay. Hawai'ian fast-lane geology at work!

At La Perouse Bay, even slight surf or swell can make entry tricky because it's rocky and slippery. Try it only in the morning when completely calm. This happens to be a local hangout, where tourists aren't necessarily appreciated. However, it's still part of the Reserve and offers good snorkeling. La Perouse often is murky, so check local conditions before trying this spot. Less experienced snorkelers would be much better off at 'Ahihi Bay.

GETTING THERE   Driving south on Highway 31, take the Wailea Iki turnoff right towards the big resorts (see map, page 83). Then turn left on Wailea Alanui Road and note the mileage at this intersection in front of The Shops at Wailea. Continue south as the road gets smaller and crosses bare lava. Pass the little bay and pass the 'Ahihi-Kina'u sign (see map, page 103). Seven miles south of the shops, you'll come to the end of the road, for non-4WD vehicles at least.

On your left will be the La Perouse Memorial monument. Just past the monument on the right is the beach with parking. Usually locals are fishing or hanging out here.

You might want to try La Perouse from one of the excursions, which can take you out where the water tends to be more clear. It is commonly murky here near the beach.

Kanaio Coast

This dramatic and beautiful black lava coast is accessible only by boat. When south swells aren't too high, there's snorkeling available in the many small coves formed when Maui's most recent lava flow produced these rugged cliffs. You could hardly find a prettier area to swim or snorkel – especially where there are dramatic black basalt columns or large lava arches in the background. Excursions such as Blue Water Rafting with their zodiac-style rafts depart from the Kihei boat ramp. A complete lack of sand in this area leaves the water more clear.

GETTING THERE   Since Highway 31 (Pi'ilani Highway) in Wailea doesn't connect with the southern section of 31, there's no way to drive to this section of the south coast. Even if the highway is ever connected, the land here is rugged enough that you couldn't reach the coast without great difficulty.

Try checking with Blue Waters Rafting for their zodiac-style rafts that can zip down here in no time (see page 132).

bottlenose dolphin

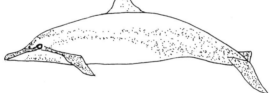

spinner dolphin

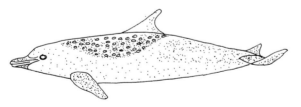

spotted dolphin

East Maui

The Hana area offers a wonderful day trip, but it's a LONG day. The Hana Highway takes almost three hours each way from Kahului, and longer when you stop a bit to enjoy the gorgeous views and waterfalls. It's an extremely slow road with countless twists and turns and very little passing, so prepare to take your time and soak in the sight of jungle greenery here on the wet side of Maui.

Hana itself is a tiny town with great charm and beautiful beaches. While you can snorkel here, the west coast is usually much calmer and more reliable, so travel to Hana for other reasons. The Seven Pools (actually more like twelve) are now called by their Hawai'ian name of 'Oheo Gulch. Waterfalls abound at 'Oheo Gulch, but so do tourists, so don't expect a fast drive on this narrow road (usually about half an hour from Hana) and don't expect seclusion. There are plenty of other pretty pools and waterfalls along the road to Hana and you may even have them to yourself. Wailua Gulch is another nice area to hike and enjoy the waterfalls. Keep in mind that Maui does have droughts that can dry up waterfalls – even on the Hana side of the island.

For beaches that are always beautiful and sometimes calm enough to snorkel, try Hana Bay, Hamoa Beach, Red Sand Beach, and Black Sand Beach in Wai'anapanapa State Park Although there are plenty of other lovely beaches, most catch the typical swells from the northeast and are seldom safe for swimming or snorkeling.

Rental car agencies all advise against driving the unpaved section of road in the far south. When we have driven it, however, the 28-mile section of graded road has been entirely adequate and virtually empty of traffic. This stretch of coast is very beautiful and in sharp contrast to the Hana Highway. It's dry, with a stark windswept beauty.

We enjoyed the lack of traffic and would recommend the road with one exception – there are practically no facilities of any sort along the road other than a couple of tiny stores that aren't always open. The rental car folks won't come out here to help you change a tire!

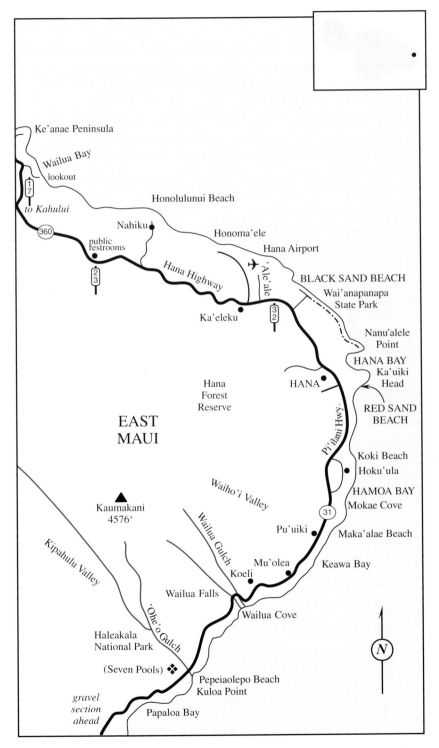

Ke'anae Peninsula

Wailua Bay

lookout

⟨1⟩⟨7⟩

to Kahului

⟨360⟩

Honolulunui Beach

Nahiku

public restrooms

Honoma'ele

Hana Airport

⟨2⟩⟨3⟩

Hana Highway

'Ale'ale

BLACK SAND BEACH

Wai'anapanapa
State Park

Ka'eleku

⟨3⟩⟨2⟩

Nanu'alele
Point

HANA BAY
Ka'uiki
Head

HANA

Hana
Forest
Reserve

Pi'ilani Hwy.

RED SAND
BEACH

EAST
MAUI

Koki Beach
Hoku'ula

HAMOA BAY
Mokae Cove

Kaumakani
4576'

Waiho'i Valley

⟨31⟩

Maka'alae Beach

Kipahulu Valley

Wailua Gulch

Pu'uiki

Mu'olea

Keawa Bay

Koeli

Wailua Falls

'Ohe'o Gulch

Wailua Cove

Haleakala
National Park

(Seven Pools) ❖

Pepeiaolepo Beach
Kuloa Point

*gravel
section
ahead*

Papaloa Bay

(N)

Hamoa Bay

As you continue on around Maui counterclockwise (not that the road connects well), the next good snorkeling is in the Hana area. Northeast swells often keep the waves and currents strong. But when swells do calm down, there is some excellent snorkeling here.

Hamoa Bay has one of Maui's most beautiful white-sand beaches in a lush location. Snorkeling is OK, but definitely not great and you need to swim out a ways to see many fish. Still, the beach is beautiful, and worth a visit – perhaps for a cool swim after the long drive to Hana.

If you decide to snorkel, head out along the left side to the protecting reef offshore. If waves and current permit, make a circle and continue on to the right side. Entry is very easy from the sand as long as the water is calm. Although we didn't see much coral, we did see sailfin tangs, rectangular triggerfish and other interesting fish. Not a bad spot for learning how to snorkel, when it is calm.

GETTING THERE   From the town of Hana, head south on the Hana Highway for one mile (see map, page 111). This is where Haneo'o Road curves off to the left looping to the water before returning to the highway. The quickest way is to take the second Haneo'o exit to the left. At four tenths of a mile from the highway, you'll see a bus stop on your right. Parking is here on the left side of the street. The stairs to Hamoa Beach are just west of the bus stop. There's a 75-yard concrete path with 21 steps down to the beach, where you'll find restrooms, showers and some food. Enter the water right at the end of the stairs for either swimming or snorkeling in this gorgeous spot.

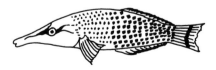

female bird wrasse

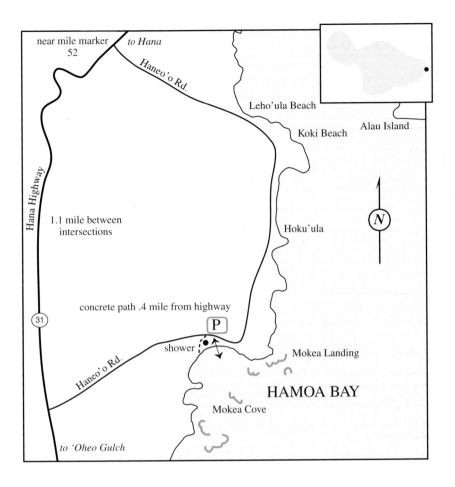

near mile marker
52

to Hana

Haneo'o Rd.

Leho'ula Beach

Koki Beach

Alau Island

Hana Highway

1.1 mile between
intersections

Hoku'ula

N

concrete path .4 mile from highway

P

shower

Haneo'o Rd.

Mokea Landing

HAMOA BAY

31

Mokea Cove

to 'Oheo Gulch

male bird wrasse

Red Sand Beach

When Hana has calm water, this beach is a special treat. The only drawback is a relatively smooth access path that looks safe, but is actually slippery and dangerous. Wear shoes with some tread (not smooth-soled flip-flops) and walk carefully to avoid slipping and sliding right over the edge. This mixture of dry powder and red lava cinder particles can work like little ball bearings. Because the path is narrow and on a steep sidehill, if you slide over the edge, you may find yourself on an unstoppable sleigh ride to the edge of a small cliff, and over down onto the rocks, and serious injury. Ouch!

The trail is popular, nevertheless, and many folks negotiate it just fine, using a little care. We like the place so much, we walk it with care. Another way in is by kayak (see page 136).

The trail just south of Hana School takes you to hidden Red Sands Beach, popular with snorkelers and nudists. Rounding the corner, the view is dramatic and spectacular. You look out upon the remains of an unusual cinder cone with a natural breakwater protecting a shallow pond. You can snorkel in the shallow water, but won't see much. The real action is through the channel outside the breakwater, where we have seen lots of bandit angelfish, schools of Moorish idols, and even a solitary reef squid (seldom seen in Maui).

Red Sand Beach is unusual, interesting, secluded, and one of our favorites. This isn't the best place for beginners or those who avoid any choppy water, but experienced snorkelers will love swimming out the channel where there's lots to see in ten to twenty-foot deep water. This outer area is protected by points further out. Keep within this outer protected bay unless the water is unusually calm and be sure to check out the view back toward the crater. No facilities.

GETTING THERE   From Hana, take Ua'kea Rd. to just past the Hana school (see map, page 115). Park here along the road and walk through the empty lot just south of the school. About 2/3 of the way back in the lot, you'll find the start of the trail on the right. An interesting old Japanese cemetery will be on your left and the bay on your right. You will also see signs warning of danger on the trail. From this point, walk slowly to avoid slipping as you wind along the edge of the sea and eventually curve to the left where you'll find Red Sand Beach at the end of the trail.

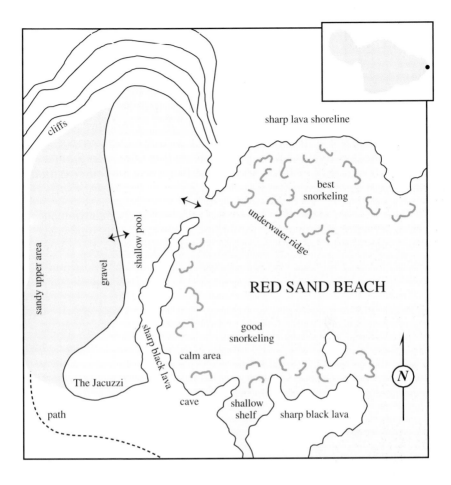

cliffs

sharp lava shoreline

best snorkeling

underwater ridge

sandy upper area

shallow pool

gravel

RED SAND BEACH

good snorkeling

sharp black lava

calm area

The Jacuzzi

cave

shallow shelf

sharp black lava

path

N

saddleback butterflyfish

Hana Bay

Hana Bay offers excellent snorkeling, when conditions are calm. The best coral lies between the old pier and the light. We prefer to enter from the sandy beach and swim right under the pier to get to the snorkeling beyond. Explore the whole area beyond the pier, checking out the areas close to the shore as well as wandering around the islands if it's calm enough there. We have seen groups of large turtles near the islands and lots of fish, coral and other critters in the protected cove just before the point.

In calm weather Hana Bay is excellent for beginners to advanced snorkelers, offers easy entry, sandy beach, showers, restrooms and even some snacks when Tutu's snack bar is open. We highly recommend snorkeling here. Those who would rather not swim far might want to consider a kayak tour with Kevin Coates (see page 136).

GETTING THERE   From the town of Hana, take Keawa Place down to the harbor (see map, page 115). Our choice is to park near the last shower on the right side of the bay. Then we have an easy entry from the sandy beach and can swim to the best snorkeling area. Alternatively, you can climb over some difficult rocks to get closer to the fish and coral right away, but it's far easier to swim. See our detail map of Hana Bay on page 115.

Fish Psychology 101

"Many fish are swimming right up and giving me dopey fish looks, which basically translate to the following statement: "Food?" That's what fish do all the time–they swim around going: "Food?" You can almost see the little questions marks over their heads. The only other thought they seem capable of is: "Yikes!"

Fish are not known for their SAT scores. This may be why they tend to do their thinking in large groups. You'll see a squadron of them coming toward you, their molecule-size brains working away on the problem ("Food?" "Food?" "Food?" "Food?"); and then you suddenly move your arm, triggering a Nuclear Fish Reaction ("Yikes!" "Yikes!" "Yikes!" "Yikes!") and FWOOOSSHH they're outta there, trailing a stream of exclamation marks.

–Dave Barry

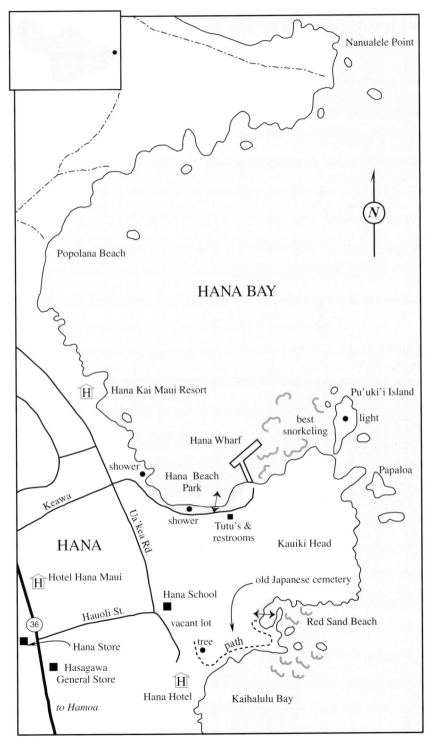

Nanualele Point

N

Popolana Beach

HANA BAY

Hana Kai Maui Resort

Pu'uki'i Island

light

best
snorkeling

Hana Wharf

Papaloa

shower

Hana Beach
Park

Keawa

Ua'Kea Rd.

shower

Tutu's &
restrooms

Kauiki Head

HANA

old Japanese cemetery

Hotel Hana Maui

Hana School

36

Hauoli St.

vacant lot

path

Red Sand Beach

Hana Store

tree

Hasagawa
General Store

Hana Hotel

Kaihalulu Bay

to Hamoa

115

Wai'anapanapa Park (Black Sand Beach)

Wai'anapanapa State Park, just north of Hana, is a beautiful place to camp with cabins, restrooms and showers available in a secluded location. Black Sand Beach (Pailoa Bay), within the park, is easy to find and worth the trip just for the pretty scenery or to picnic. It is often too rough for safe snorkeling. When calm enough, you can snorkel quite a ways to the right – even snorkel through a large natural arch. It's a pretty swim and you'll find some small coral and fish, but not nearly as much as Hana Bay. The view of a huge rock arch from the water is spectacular, and the swim under it (if the tide is not high) is thrilling and dramatic. You'll know you're not in Kansas anymore.

Beginners can enjoy the beach, the view and a quick dip, while experienced snorkelers may want to try this for the novelty. Enjoy the beauty of the lava formations at this lovely park. You may also want to hike some of the King's Highway heading south along the coast – still within the state park.

GETTING THERE   The entrance to Waianapanapa State Park is located along the Hana Highway (Highway 360) near mile marker 32 (see map, page 116) and has a large sign. The paved road with speed bumps takes you straight to the office at four tenths of a mile. At this junction the road to the right heads toward the cabins, while the one to the left heads to Black Sand Beach. Park at the end of the road where it hits the sea and you'll be able to look down to view Black Sands Beach.

To the right will be restrooms, showers and a paved path down to the beach. The path takes you to the beach where the inner cove is fairly well protected. Entry is easy in calm water.

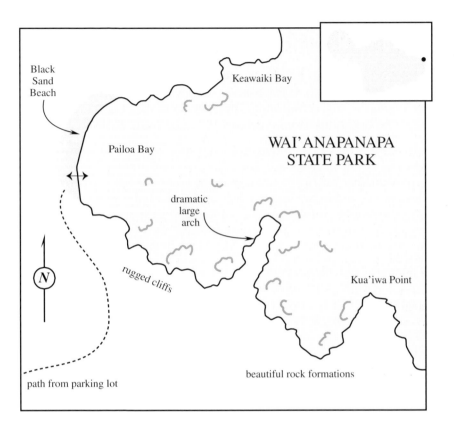

Black
Sand
Beach

Keawaiki Bay

Pailoa Bay

WAI'ANAPANAPA
STATE PARK

dramatic
large
arch

N

rugged cliffs

Kua'iwa Point

path from parking lot

beautiful rock formations

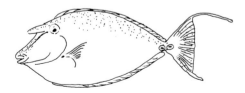

unicornfish

Molokini Island

Molokini Island has become something of a legend – almost a mythical destination. It is certainly heavily advertised and promoted as a fantastic snorkeling spot. There's truth in this, but it's hard to separate the reality from the hype. How good is it, really?

Molokini is indeed a unique and interesting place, well worth visiting. A few decades ago, it had lots of coral and fish. Unfortunately, hurricane damage to the coral has left expanses of dead coral, and hence smaller fish counts. Still, the snorkeling is good, visibility almost always excellent and getting there takes you on a beautiful trip along the coast of Maui. This is also an excellent site for beginners and children. Most folks love their Molokini trip.

There are large numbers of excursions to choose from, so select your departure point, type of boat (if that's important to you), and a quality trip, if you care about the food, if you plan to dive or Snuba, or if you're a beginner and want good supervision and help. We didn't see as many fish or nearly as much coral as we had expected (the hype had given us unrealistic expectations), but the variety of fish was excellent. The inside of the crater has little coral on the floor, but plenty of large, almost tame fish. We did see lots of eels.

It can be somewhat choppy here even on the inside, since it's almost open ocean. Your excursion can offer life vests, inner tubes, or whatever it takes to make your experience easier. This is a perfect place to try the snorkels designed to keep choppy water out (even more true later in the day).

Although there can be dozens of boats lined up inside the crater, it's a big place, and everyone seems to fit. Once you're in the water snorkeling, it doesn't seem crowded unless you stay near the boat. With more boats sharing the crater, we find they tend to restrict your available area – after all, the responsible excursions want to keep an eye on all their snorkelers. Even within the designated area, we have seen plenty of butterflyfish, bird wrasses, parrotfish, Moorish idols, tangs, triggerfish, and eels.

If your excursion happens to anchor at the edge of the crater, be very cautious before venturing past the point of the crater. Strong currents are common at both outer edges of the island. Go there only with good supervision no matter how well you swim.

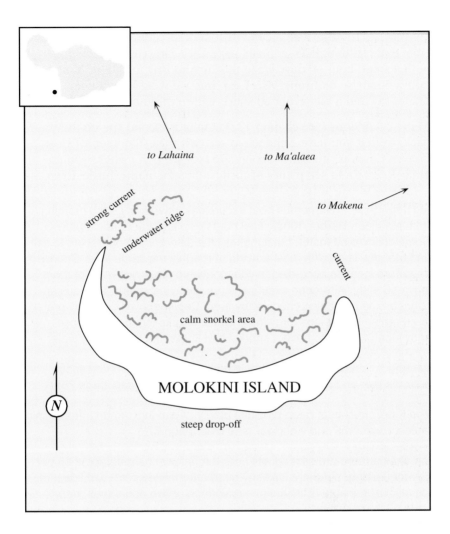

to Lahaina

to Ma'alaea

to Makena

strong current

underwater ridge

current

calm snorkel area

MOLOKINI ISLAND

steep drop-off

N

For an unusual experience, tag along with a dive boat or take a smaller excursion to see the dramatic back side, with its sheer cliffs. The back sometimes has strong currents, so can be beyond the abilities of even the best swimmers. Carefully supervised drift dives are the best way to see the back side. For snorkeling, the back is similar in terms of coral and fish (though you're looking mainly at a wall). It's completely uncrowded and even more dramatic with the sheer wall on one side and the deepest blue water on the other. Do NOT attempt to swim there from the inner crater! There can be killer currents at both points of Molokini – good for a free trip to Tahiti.

We particularly like a chance to drift snorkel along the inner crater edge that's submerged (see map, page 119). This can only be done with a small boat on days when the current isn't too swift. Your captain will advise and supervise. Last time we were here we saw a manta ray and a white-tipped shark within minutes – quite a thrill.

Many excursions (see chapter 122) stop at a second site on the way back, so that you have a chance to see two sites. The reef off Five Graves/Caves is often the second site (see page 91) where you are almost certain to see plenty of turtles, thus the name Turtle Town.

GETTING THERE
Numerous boat excursions leave early each morning from Ma'alaea Harbor, Kihei small boat ramp and the Lahaina pier. Some claim to be faster, but it makes little difference. You get out to sea and the race is on with most arriving at roughly the same time. Choose departure location according to your convenience, since most of them leave so early. Afternoon excursions are always cheaper, but you can count on the sea being choppier by then. Beginners will definitely prefer the morning excursions for calmer, easier snorkeling. If you choose afternoon, it's best to have a snorkel that keeps out the choppy water.

Parking is fairly easy at Ma'alaea, where you can find parking space near the pier and can drive right up to any boat (see map, page 75).

The Kihei small boat ramp provides plenty of parking, shade trees, picnic tables, restrooms and a shower (see map, page 77).

In Lahaina there are several lots near the harbor charging about $6 per day for parking, but there isn't any good alternative since roadside parking all over Lahaina is limited to a maximum of two hours (see map, page 69).

At all three departure points, you can drop passengers and gear near the boat, so one of you can check in while another parks. Some excursions also ask that you check in at their office and pick up snorkeling gear before heading for the boat.

trumpetfish

Motion Sickness

Motion sickness (seasickness or carsickness) is a minor inner ear disorder which can really cut into your pleasure on the water, on long, curvy road trips or in choppy air. Fortunately, motion sickness is quite controllable these days. All it takes is a little advance planning to turn a potentially miserable experience into a normal, fun one. Don't let old fears keep you from great water adventures anymore.

Mel can get seasick just by vividly imagining a rocking boat, so he has tried just about every remedy personally. These field trials are a messy business, so we'll spare you the details, and just pass on what really works in our experience.

Forget the wrist pressure-point bands – they don't do the job for anyone we've ever met. You might as well put them in the closet along with your ultrasonic pest repeller, in our opinion.

The most effective remedy we've found so far is Meclizine, a pill available by prescription only. It works perfectly for Mel with no noticeable side effects. Alcohol can interact with it to make you drowsy. We learned about Meclizine when Jon Carroll, a columnist in the San Francisco Chronicle, reported that it had sufficed for him in 15-25' swells on the way to Antarctica. If it does the job there, it should handle all but the most radical of snorkeling excursions.

An over-the-counter alternative is Benadryl usually used as a decongestant. It can also be effective against motion sickness. Ginger is also used but may not be strong enough for some people.

Use these medicines carefully and only after consulting your doctor. In some cases, you must avoid alcohol, other drugs or diving, since these medications can produce drowsiness.

Maui Excursions

We like the advantages of snorkeling shore-accessible sites, and that's the main focus of this book. If you have a rental car, you can get up on your own schedule, and for the cost of a little gas have a great Hawai'ian outdoor adventure with your whole family.

It would be a mistake, however, to never sample the incredible smorgasbord of excursions available on Maui. Excursions can take you to places only accessible by boat. Step on to a beautiful boat in the morning, and you are taken care of with food and drinks and fun things to do for many hours. There are some advantages to boat-entry snorkeling, particularly if the swell is up – slip right into the water without dealing with sand and surf or long swims. As much as we love shore snorkeling, we intersperse excursions as a spice in our explorations and get to know Maui better in the process.

Maui is just loaded with excursion possibilities – far more than we could review here. The reviews we've chosen to include were all excursions we enjoyed personally, in some cases so much we've gone on them several times. We've tried to include as much variety as possible – from small to large, from simple and cheap to deluxe with all the extras. You could spend several vacations doing nothing but working your way through every Molokini excursion, but we've only included a few sample trips that seemed especially appealing. The ones we include are trips that our fellow passengers also enjoyed.

We've included prices when available to give you an idea of the range, but always keep in mind that prices do change, and may be higher by the time you read this. Companies change ownership or go out of business regularly in this competitive location, so always call first to double check on all the details. We've tried to include Maui's best excursions to excellent sites and expect these companies are more likely to remain in business.

While we can't speak for all available excursions, the ones in this book seem to be responsible about your safety and making sure you get your money's worth. For that reason, they often need to change course for the day depending on the captain's latest information about wind, swell and visibility There's no need to be disappointed if you don't end up exactly where you expected. It's more important that you snorkel in good conditions where you can relax and have a great time.

Tipping the crew is common in Maui and crews are not likely to refuse a bit of cash. While you may think these crew members have the world's best jobs, they still have to pay the high Hawai'ian cost of living. If you're inclined to tip, bring along some extra cash.

Most excursions do not give refunds unless you cancel at least 24 hours ahead, regardless of the weather (barring hurricanes). You may wake up in the morning, it's raining or windy, and you think the trip won't go out. Yet, by the time you're out and to the site, the sun may have come out. Expect your excursion to go out even if the weather doesn't seem ideal to you – most captains tell us that they miss very few days all year. This is a good reason to choose a company you trust – one that will assure a safe and happy experience.

Trilogy

This well-run company operates five first-class racing catamarans. Their excursions go out to Molokini Crater from Ma'alaea Harbor (see map, page 75), to Lana'i from Lahaina Harbor (see map, page 69), and to Lana'i sites from the Manele Bay Resort (page 145). They can arrange packages with overnight stays in Lana'i.

Two trips leave Lahaina for Lana'i. The first is for early risers eager to enjoy the calm morning conditions at Hulopo'e Bay. The later departure stays well into the afternoon. The newest trip leaves from Ka'anapali Beach. These are top-of-the-line excursions and priced accordingly, but they work hard to make every detail first class. You're likely to enjoy any of the Trilogy excursions, if your budget allows.

All Trilogy excursions begin with coffee, tea, cocoa, fruit, juice and their own freshly-baked gourmet cinnamon rolls. Yummy! Various soft drinks and juices fill the coolers for you to help yourself. Alcoholic drinks aren't stocked, but you may bring your own and keep it in their cooler for use only after your snorkeling is done.

Lunches, whether grilled on board or on shore, usually include their delicious marinated chicken. Champagne and ice cream accompany your return voyage on some trips.

Scuba and introductory dives are available for an additional cost. Crew members always seem happy, helpful and hard-working. They manage to create an understated, yet deluxe experience, casual but impeccably detailed.

Trilogy is only allowed to use the Hulopo'e Bay beach on weekdays. On weekends and holidays, they run a Lana'i trip called "Seafari". You sail along the south side of Lana'i to snorkel at Cathedrals or Shark Fin Rock. Then back to the Manele Bay Harbor for lunch and an island tour if you wish. Various add-ons appeal to repeat customers.

The catamarans are beautiful, although be prepared for little shade on all except Trilogy I. They always sail at least part of the way, winds permitting, and it is exhilarating to see these sleek boats knifing through the waves, with the only sounds the gurgle of your wake and the flapping of the sails.

Trilogy is always well-organized, so you don't have to worry about a thing. We've sampled all their excursions and notice that everyone seems to have a great time. See our Lana'i chapter for more information about these destinations.

The Molokini trip costs $94.39 with tax for an adult. Lahaina to Lana'i is $168.80. The trip from Ka'anapali is $94.39. Children ages 3-12 are half price; those under 3 go for free.

Trilogy	800-188-9800
trilogy@maui.net	808-661-4743
www.trilogy.com	808-667-7766 fax

Navatek II

This large and comfortable ship cruises over to the Lana'i site Cathedrals in two hours from Lahaina Harbor. It leaves promptly at 9:00 a.m. and returns at 3:00 p.m. The ship rides high in the water on its special pontoons and is remarkably smooth. If you want a more protected, big-boat ride than sailing catamarans offer, Navatek II fits the bill. It holds 120 people, so it's best if you like company.

One of Navatek's specialties is a hot breakfast, featuring lavish waffles with strawberries, whipped cream and much more, served buffet-style in the main cabin. After a decent interval to eat, the crew members are introduced and various activities explained. This is somewhat more like a cruise ship event, as they let you in on all the activities and personnel available, including naturalist, photographer, Scuba, Snuba, Hawai'ian crafts, tales of Lana'i history and legends, and even massage ($15 for 15 minutes). You can watch the excellent video, check out the fish ID books, or laze in the sun or shade up on the large deck with plenty of lounge chairs.

Leaving Maui we were immediately treated to the sight of three bottlenose dolphins swimming and leaping just inches in front of the boat as we sped along. Cruising by Lana'i, we saw numerous little flying fish near the boat.

We had an excellent hour and a half snorkel at the Cathedrals site, where we saw octopus, eels, peacock flounder, saddleback butterflyfish, and more. Cathedrals lies along the sheer cliffs of southern Lana'i – a spectacular setting.

As is often the case on large boats, Scuba and Snuba people entered the water first from the easy steps, so snorkelers get to wait unless they are willing and able to jump in from the side. Restrooms were larger, cleaner and more numerous than on smaller boats. A warm water shower after snorkeling was wonderful, making it possible to change out of salty clothes and be even more comfortable for the trip back to Maui.

Snuba costs extra and is available for ages eight and up. The video is excellent quality. Good-quality underwater cameras are $27. The naturalist was knowledgeable and always available to help. She brought along plenty of interesting books and exhibits.

Lunch is buffet-style and includes chicken, hamburgers, pasta, salad with sodas and alcoholic drinks of all sorts readily available throughout the trip. Cookies and ice cream on the return voyage complete the picture. If your style is "one of each, please", you'll wind up more than satisfied: stuffed and sozzled, too.

Our only complaint (as advanced snorkelers and curious wanderers) was that they set boundaries rather close to the ship, guarded by crew on surfboards, and granted no exemptions. It was all in the name of safety, as there was a small surge near the rocks, but it felt overly rigid and made us feel a bit herded.

This is one of the more expensive trips available, but it's a good one if you're looking for a cheery cruise ship atmosphere. This trip (including tax) runs $115 for an adult, $95 for ages 12 to adult, $75 for ages 5-11. Bring your AAA card for a 20% discount.

Navatek   808-873-3475

Expeditions Ferry

The Lahaina-Lana'i passenger ferry, called Expeditions, offers five trips each way per day from Lahaina Harbor to Manele Harbor on Lana'i. Fares are $50 round trip for adults; $40 for children 2 through 11; children under 2 are free on your lap. The compact, seaworthy ferry starts at 6:45 a.m. each day from Lahaina and takes about 45 minutes to Manele Harbor. The last return trip is at 6:45 p.m.

You may add car, jeep, golf or an overnight stay in Lana'i to the package. Bring lots of paper or plastic money if you plan on staying, as there are no inexpensive options other than camping or one small hotel in Lana'i City.

Consider creating your own delightful day trip that requires walking just five minutes from the Manele Bay Harbor to Hulopo'e Beach in front of the Manele Bay Hotel. Take a picnic lunch or splurge at the award-winning Manele Bay Resort. Facilities such as enclosed showers, restrooms, water, shade and picnic tables are all available on the beach and at the harbor. Sip coffee on the first ferry of the day out of Lahaina, live it up on Lana'i, then enjoy the romantic view of Maui's lights on your evening return. For more details about this destination, see our section about Lana'i beginning on page 144. We highly recommend this day trip – especially when there is little south swell.

Expeditions Ferry   808-661-3756

Club Lana'i

Those who have been visiting Maui for years may remember the eight-acre Club Lana'i facility that operated independently on the east coast of Lana'i, and provided a funky Gilligan's Island-like day trip that was unique. Alas, the Club property was sold and seems destined to become another luxury condominium development.

Now, the old Club Lana'i boats are offering snorkeling trips to various sites around Lana'i – including The Club, Armchair, Stone Shack and Manele Bay Harbor on the eastern side of Lana'i. They usually snorkel at least two of these sites depending on swells and visibility. Captains always have the final say as to their destination and will consult with each other as well as scout out the sites.

The folks operating Club Lana'i and its ships have always been friendly and casual. Don't expect deluxe or too many extras, but do expect lower prices and an enjoyable trip. The day starts with juice

126

Discounts

Discounts are available for many excursions. If you're so inclined, a little work and the right questions can save you a fair chunk of change. Begin by picking up one of the numerous free promotional magazines such as Maui Gold. These are readily available at the airport, hotels and shops. They usually include special offers, coupons and other deals to attract customers.

Calling an excursion office and asking if there are any special offers can sometimes pay off, especially when tourism is slower. Summer and holidays the ships fill more quickly, but there is still plenty of competition on Maui, so it's always worth a try.

Ships often charge less for children and nothing for toddlers. Each ship has its own definition of child and adult. Don't hesitate to ask about senior discounts, repeat customer discounts, and kama'aina rate (if you live in the islands and can prove it by showing your driver's license). Sometimes discounts are provided to AAA members.

For discounts ranging from 10-20%, try Activity World in Lahaina. They buy blocks of tickets and can mail tickets to the mainland. They're also open every day of the year from 7 a.m. until 9 p.m. They're located at 888 Wainee, Suite 130. Call (800) 624-7771 or 667-7777 in Maui. Last-minute tickets are also sometimes offered at an even better price. This is helpful if you are flexible, but not so useful if your vacation time is in short supply.

For a free trip, sign up for a timeshare offer. You will have to sit through an hour or two of sales talk in exchange for your bargain trip. Do not underestimate their sales ability!

When you do book tickets ahead of time and charge them to your credit card, remember that when the ship goes out with or without you, you will be charged for the trip. The fine print usually requires you to cancel at least 24 hours ahead. You may wake up to weather that doesn't suit you only to find that the ship sailed anyway, and you will get to pay as agreed. Often your destination isn't guaranteed. You might have your heart set on Molokini only to find the ship change to Makena Landing due to rough weather. This does not entitle you to cancel. Keep in mind they do have to make changes for safety reasons so go with the flow.

or coffee and several types of pound cake right after you depart from the Lahaina Harbor. Lunch is build-your-own deli sandwiches, pasta, salad, sodas and beer.

Call to find out which trips Club Lana'i is offering currently.

Club Lana'i   808-871-1144

Ultimate Rafting Eco Tours & Ultimate Whale Watch

Departing from Lahaina Harbor, Ultimate Rafting takes small groups on either four or six-hour snorkel and wildlife viewing tours to Lana'i, aboard a high-performance inflatable boat. Their boat is speedy so the trip to Lana'i takes only twenty minutes if there's no detour to watch whales. All snorkeling equipment and instruction are provided. Snacks, drinks and lunch (served onboard) are simple, but good. The ride can be very bumpy, so it isn't a good choice for anyone with back problems or for pregnant women. Trips vary depending on weather conditions, so call for details.

A bit of snorkeling experience will help if you want to fully appreciate the wonderful sites they visit. This is a delightful experience for the snorkeler who can handle a wet bumpy trip, lack of restroom and perhaps choppy water offshore at Lana'i. They have plenty of sites from which to choose since Lana'i is nearly surrounded by reef.

We traveled with ten other snorkelers and all were delighted with the trip. Besides the great snorkeling, we were treated to the sight of the first humpback whale of the season, spotted dolphins and spinner dolphins that jumped so close to the boat that they thoroughly splashed us. With or without the dolphins, you're likely

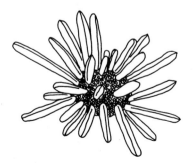

slatepencil sea urchin

to get wet, so come prepared for sun and water. In the winter you might want a good windbreaker that works when wet. Forget hats without a strap because they'll end up in the channel immediately.

Ultimate Rafting is owned and operated by marine biologists who focus on the whales in season. We highly recommend this trip for adventuresome and reasonably sturdy snorkelers who enjoy a smaller group. And we recommend the six-hour trip because it can get you to some more remote and beautiful snorkeling sites on the back (west) of Lana'i – traveling around the whole island if weather permits.

We loved the trip around Lana'i and enjoyed snorkeling Twin Palms (where we saw lots of turtles and extensive reefs), Shark Fin Rock (where we saw schools of butterflyfish in gin-clear water under the tallest cliffs on Lana'i) and Coral Gardens (tiny, but full of fish). The crew members were informative and helpful.

Food was a morning snack and well as lots of mini-sandwiches and potato salad for lunch. Plenty of water, sodas and (after swimming) beer were available. Gear, of course, was provided. You get a lot of sun exposure in six hours mid-day, so plan ahead to avoid later headaches. This is adventure eco-tourism!

Ultimate Rafting   808-667-5678
ecoraft@maui.net

Eco-Adventures (Pacific Whale Foundation)

Eco-Adventures is the excursion arm of Pacific Whale Foundation, a noteworthy contributor to marine conservation in Maui. In addition to their focus on whales, they are involved in coral reef research. All profits from Eco-Adventures goes to marine conservation.

From Lahaina, their trips head to Lana'i. From Ma'alaea, the trips head to Molokini and Lana'i. All gear, instructions, food and drinks are provided. Some of their excursions charge $2 for alcoholic drinks. When departing from Lahaina, you will need to meet at their store at 143 Dickenson Street to pick up snorkeling gear before walking down to the Lahaina Harbor.

We took their distinctive-looking large silver boat Ocean Explorer from Lahaina Harbor. Seating on this boat is in comfortable canvas deck-type chairs and the boat is fairly roomy with storage under your seat. Restrooms, stairs into the water, ample beverages and food all contribute to an enjoyable trip. The day starts with muffins, juice, fruit and coffee – what they call a tropical breakfast. Lunch is make-your-own deli sandwiches.

The day we joined this excursion there were only 12 snorkelers in all, so we had plenty of access to the helpful crew members, who were full of information – especially about whales and dolphins. Having top staff like Captain Tom Allen, who lived on Lana'i for six years (and contributed many details for our Lana'i section), is a real plus. Our snorkeling stops were Summerhouse (near The Club) and Manele Harbor (just south of the boat traffic). Summerhouse was 10-15 feet deep with extensive coral and many turtles. Manele Harbor is a smaller area, but has an unusually large number of fish.

This trip offers personal attention, a low-key atmosphere and all the comfort you might need. This is a responsible, well-run outfit that we highly recommend – not as small as the rafts, but considerably more spacious, shady and comfortable; not nearly as large or expensive as the big guys, but more personal.

Prices range from $49 for an afternoon trip to $89 for a longer trip on the Ocean Explorer. These prices are for adults plus tax. Children are ages 4-12. For most of their excursions, children under 4 are free. Tipping is not allowed.

Pacific Whale Fdn.   800-WHALE-1-1
cruises@pacificwhale.org   808-879-8811
www.pacificwhale.org

Reef Dancer

A glass-bottom/side boat (which they describe as semi-submersible; not a submarine) boarding from Lahaina Harbor at slip #10. Rates are $32.95 plus tax per adult and $18.95 for children 6-12. The large windows wrap under and to the side allowing a wide view. With a detailed narrative, this offers a chance to learn about the underwater world without getting wet. Reef Dancer offers five tours daily. Call for the current schedule.

Reef Dancer   888-667-2133
                     808-667-2133
www.galaxymall.com/stores/reefdancer

Atlantis

Atlantis pioneered viewing the underwater world from real, scaled-down submarines. Their Maui submarine trip leaves from the Lahaina Harbor. Check in at the Pioneer Inn on Front Street directly across from the pier.

The view is through portholes, because this is a real submarine, which takes you down to 100 feet deep. Prices are $79 per adult and $39 for ages 12 or less. The excursion takes about two hours total, because you need to take a boat trip out to board the sub. The submarine ride itself lasts about 45 minutes.It's educational and lots of fun for those who don't want to actually get in the water.

Atlantis   808-667-2224

Pride of Maui

Located at Ma'alaea Harbor, ready to sprint for Molokini. This is a sleek and speedy 65-foot catamaran with indoor space for seating and gear, but lots more room on the sunny, upper deck where all the activities center. Since Pride of Maui attracts lots of young fun and sun seekers, it's a party!

The fun starts with a continental breakfast – in this case a choice of muffins, fruit, coffee, and fruit punch.

The trip to Molokini is smooth and comfortable. The crew sets boundaries for snorkeling at Molokini, although they don't seem overly rigid about them. With so many boats anchored here at once, it isn't surprising that they try hard to keep an eye on all their charges.

Lunch is ample, with a choice of chicken (which disappears fast), huge hamburgers, grilled fish with plenty of salads, soft drinks and beer. The second snorkeling site is often "Turtle Town" just offshore from the Maui Prince Hotel, a beautiful spot indeed. Scuba and Snuba were offered here for an extra charge. At this site divers may glimpse a frogfish or perhaps the elusive green leaf scorpionfish.

Depending on the weather, the second site can sometimes be off Olowalu. Both of these second sites are good, and can be just as much fun as Molokini. All in all, a most pleasant, relaxing way to see some of the best that Maui has to offer. Pride of Maui charges $70 (including tax) per adult for the morning trip, $40 for ages 5-12, $60 for ages 13-18. The afternoon trip is only $40 per adult and $20 for ages 5-12, but offers only one stop and choppier water. This doesn't go out every day, so call first. Keep in mind that afternoon trips might be diverted to La Perouse or Coral Gardens, so (as with any excursion) go in the morning if your heart is set on Molokini.

Pride of Maui   808-875-0955

Blue Water Rafting

Blue Water Rafting stands out as the pioneer of adventure rafting trips to the dramatic Kanaio Coast. The Kanaio coast is located at the southern part of Maui, south of Makena, with spectacular lava formations. Blue Water operates trips to Molokini, Kanaio Sea Caves, whale watching, snorkel combo trips and charters. Their Zodiac-type boats hold from 6 to 20 people. For trips to the Kanaio Coast, you may choose either four hours or 5 1/2 hours.

Trips leave on the early side (about 7:30 a.m.) from the Kihei public boat ramp. Their high-performance boat can reach the spectacular cliffs of the Kanaio Coast early enough to allow about four stops for snorkeling and eating (and still return at about 1:00 p.m.).

Some bench seating is available near the back (where the ride is a bit smoother), but most is around the side tubes of the raft. The side seats provide the best sense of closeness to the water and speed. They are popular! Ropes are provided and all passengers must hold on while the boat is moving – a sensible policy. There's no need to rush for a seat, since they make sure everyone is comfortable. Just speak up if you don't want to sit at the bow of the boat. There will surely be someone who thinks that's the best seat in town.

Like the other raft trips in Maui, this is not the best for pregnant women or anyone with much of a back problem because they WILL deliver a bouncy ride. You can count on a wild ride (even on a calm day), so come prepared to enjoy the ride and get wet. While they have storage for all your gear, it's hard to keep anything completely dry on a trip like this. A waterproof bag for your expensive camera might be good insurance.

You can also count on getting plenty of sun, so sunscreen and/or cover-ups are necessary. There are a few shady seats behind the captain, but the awning won't keep off the reflected rays of the sun.

That said, it's a terrific trip – one that you'll be wanting to try again. Everyone on our trip was absolutely delighted even though we were out on a south-swell day – not the easiest when you're heading for the south coast. The captain's decision that day was to cruise the Kanaio Coast to check out its unique beauty – these arches, caves, waterspouts, basalt columns and lava cliffs are not something you can reach from land. Then, we headed back to calmer waters for snorkeling.

This small boat was able to do three sites at Molokini – far more interesting than just the usual inner area. When we did a drift snorkel (a slow, safe drift) along the submerged rim of Molokini, we had the unusual treat of seeing a manta ray and a white-tipped shark in the first few minutes! We also stopped briefly to bob up and down in the big swell along the back of Molokini, where we had a peek at the deep indigo of the much deeper water. Safe fun!

A snack and lunch were served onboard while the boat stopped in a pretty, calm spot. Food was fix-your-own deli sandwiches, fruit, muffins, and plenty of drinks (not alcoholic) with ample amounts of everything. The rafts do not have restrooms, but there were plenty of chances to hop off the raft. Getting in and out of the water is easy with no waiting in line since you can slide down the side with ease. A ladder is available when you return.

Quality gear and patient help was available for all. The captain and crew member also provided interesting information about the area where we traveled. The atmosphere with Blue Water Rafting is both informative and entertaining, casual and responsible, and most of all, great fun.

Blue Water Rafting   808-879-RAFT
www.BlueWaterRafting.com

Dive Boats

PADI and NAUI attempt to regulate the diving industry with strict rules, since there are serious risks involved. No one is allowed to dive without certification (a C card). Anyone who wants to dive without proper training is certainly a fool, and the shops who will take such rash people out are equally foolish. We have seen excursions all over the world offering to take people down without proof of certification. This is not the mark of the highest level of safety consciousness. Keep in mind that other advice and services from such operators may be similarly casual. Always take extra care with any rental equipment.

When their business is slow, some take divers (or snorkelers) to sites they can't handle. On the better snorkeling excursions, they keep a close eye on all their charges, so it's like having a lifeguard along.

With a dive boat you may find yourself on the surface as a snorkeler in much rougher conditions than the divers 60 feet beneath you. You'll need to rely on a buddy since the crew is usually more focused on the divers.

South Pacific Kayaks & Outfitters

Kayaking is an interesting and different way to get out on the water, and allows access to some snorkeling spots that are difficult or impossible to reach any other way.

Kayaking tours, kayak rentals (with attachment for your car), sales and service are all offered at South Pacific's Kihei location in the Rainbow Mall (see map, page 77). They are a well-established operation with an extensive array of environment-friendly excursions available to all activity levels and ages. This is a wonderful way to enjoy the waters of Maui without the crowds.

All of their trips offer single or double kayaks, complete snorkeling gear, snacks, drinks, and sometimes lunch as well. Snorkeling can be from the coastline or from the kayak.

The Marine Reserve Explorer trip (their longest snorkeling trip, $89 plus tax for an adult) is small and far more personal than most boat excursions. Meet at 6:20 a.m. at the office in Kihei and they take care of the rest. The trip begins in the south (near La Perouse) and continues north along the 'Ahihi-Kina'u coast – a beautiful area with excellent hard-to-reach snorkeling. Our stops included Aquarium, where we saw an octopus, dolphins and rays.

The second stop was Fish Pond, a tiny bay protected by a breakwater – perfect for beginning snorkelers. A delicious deli lunch was served here on the beach. Our third stop was 'Ahihi Bay, another excellent, easy snorkeling site with turtles in residence.

Each kayaking stint was fairly short and easy, only about fifteen minutes, although could take much longer in bad weather. The hardest part was lifting the kayaks in and out of the water, walking on lava (arduous even with the guide's help). Be sure to tell them if you can't help with this. Since the group is small and the guide is patient, timing is relaxed.

Don't underestimate how much sun you will get in a kayak! Bring sunscreen, T-shirt, broad-brimmed hat and sunglasses. This is a unique, quiet, delightful way to see some of Maui's best sites.

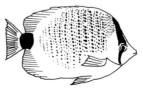

milletseed butterflyfish

Other trips include Turtle Reef in the Makena area ($59 for adults), good for families with young or inexperienced kayakers They also have a new 'Ahihi Bay trip starting out at the northern end of 'Ahihi Bay and offering a challenge to more experienced kayakers. During whale season, imagine the thrill of viewing whales eye to eye from a kayak (Whale Watch $59 per adult). For West Maui visitors they depart from Olowalu or Ukemehame (Ukemehame Snorkel Safari for $59).

Call to be updated on current excursions since they can easily change itinerary – especially when weather and wave direction changes.

Kihei office at 2439 S. Kihei Rd. in the Rainbow Mall.

South Pacific Kayaks   808-875-4848
seakayak@maui.net   800-776-2326
  808-875-4691 fax

Snorkel Maui

Perhaps you wish you could go out snorkeling with some local folks who just happen to be marine biology experts. Well, you can: Ann Fielding and Sue Robinson provide individualized, informative snorkeling tours with shore entry. Ann is a well-known marine biologist, and author of one of our favorite reference books, "An Underwater Guide to Hawai'i". Sue is a professional diver and underwater photographer headquartered in Maui.

Sites vary depending on local weather and waves. Sue or Ann escort you to special sites they know well and can take you to see fish friends of theirs that hang out in specific spots. Call to check when the next trip is scheduled or make your own arrangements with them. They take a maximum of 6 people and cater to your particular needs and abilities. Tell them if you are a beginner or plan to bring children because they can have special equipment available.

The day we joined Sue, our first stop was the parking lot just south of 'Ahihi Cove. Shoes or booties were needed for the short hike down to the beach. We sat in a beautiful and secluded spot at the edge of the rocky beach, learning about the geology of the Hawai'ian islands as well as reef building and the story of Hawai'ian coral and fish. She then led us on a guided snorkeling tour of the area, pointing out such beauties as male and female bird wrasses, oval butterflyfish, Heller's barracuda, razor coral, a white-mouth moray, blue-stripe butterflyfish, fantail tang and fish-cleaning stations.

Our second stop was the little park at the south end of the Maui Prince Hotel, where we relaxed with muffins and juice before another guided snorkel to see some of the many turtles and fish at this reef.

This is a wonderful and most unusual opportunity to have far better personal attention than the large tour boats can provide. Sue and Ann can help you learn to use your gear, teach you to differentiate the kinds of Hawai'ian coral, or simply provide a safe and fun way to introduce children to the precious resources of Hawai'ian reefs. Their emphasis is on education and tailoring the experience to each person's interests and abilities.

Snorkel Maui	800-635-1273
Ann Fielding	808-572-8437
Sue Robinson	808-879-3584

Kayak Hana Bay

Stop by Hana Bay Harbor most days and you'll find Kevin Coates set up at the side of the road near the harbor with his array of kayaks available for rent. He sells kayaks as well as renting them by the hour. Better yet, consider a guided snorkeling tour. He provides the kayaks, snorkeling equipment and takes you to some of Hana's best snorkeling sites – assuming weather permits. This is a nice way for beginners to give snorkeling a try with plenty of personal help.

If you want to snorkel off Red Sand Beach without the hike, ask Kevin if conditions are calm enough that he can guide you there by kayak. None of these sites require a long paddle. The cost is $59 plus tax for each adult. When the conditions are good for snorkeling, look for Kevin near the stack of kayaks right across from the beach at Hana Bay (see map, page 115). After 9:00 in the morning, or 2:00 in the afternoon, he may be out guiding a few snorkelers.

Kayak Hana Bay   808-248-7711

Snuba Tours of Maui

While we haven't tried this excursion on Maui, we're tried Snuba on other islands and like it. See Snuba, page 192.

Snuba Tours of Maui   808-879-8410

Snuba

Snuba was developed as a simpler alternative to Scuba for shallow dives in resort conditions. Because Snuba divers are strictly limited in depth and conditions, and always accompanied by an instructor, training takes just 15-30 minutes. Two people share a small inflatable raft, which holds a Scuba air tank. A twenty-foot hose leads from the tank to a light harness on each diver. A soft, light weight belt completes your outfit. Very light and tropical!

Once in the water, your instructor teaches you to breathe through your regulator (which has a mouthpiece just like your snorkel) on the surface until you're completely comfortable. You're then free to swim around as you like -- only down to twenty feet deep, of course. The raft will automatically follow you as you tour the bay.

It's that easy! You have to be at least eight years old, and have normal good health. Kids do amazingly well, and senior citizens can also enjoy Snuba.

We are certified Scuba divers, yet we tried Snuba because this was a perfect place to see what made it special. It actually has some advantages over Scuba in that you're free of the cumbersome equipment. There's none of the macho attitude you sometimes see on dive boats.

Snuba strikes us as a fun reasonably safe experience if you pay attention and use it according to directions. Where the reef is shallow, and conditions calm, it can actually be better than diving because you're so unencumbered in the water.

Warning: pay attention to the instructions because even at these shallow depths, you must know the proper way to surface. You must remember to never hold your breath as you ascend or you could force a bubble of air into your blood. Breathing out continually while surfacing is not intuitive, but absolutely necessary when you're breathing compressed air. This is especially important to remember if you're used to surface diving where you always hold your breath.

Enjoy and dive safely!

Land Excursions

Maui Ocean Center

Maui's new aquarium, located in Ma'alaea near the harbor, is open 9-5 daily. This five-acre park host 60 delightful exhibits – including jellyfish, tiger shark, octopus, spotted eagle rays, green sea turtles and the colorful living reef. Emphasis is on endemic creatures of Hawai'i, so this is a perfect opportunity to see what the waters around you have to offer. The eight-foot tiger shark in the walk-through display is a crowd pleaser, but other tiny creatures are just as fascinating. Come early because time passes quickly when you're trying to see it all. The exhibits are located both inside and outside.

Free parking is provided and you can also enjoy the restaurant, cafe and gift shop. For location, see map page 75.

Maui Ocean Center   808-270-7000
192 Ma'alaea Road

Haleakala Crater

Driving up nearly to the top of Maui is a popular way to view the sunrise (see map, page 139). The crater is spectacular and huge. Keep in mind that it will be quite cold at nearly 10,000' so bring warm clothing. Great hiking trails await, but the altitude takes some getting used to. Don't try too much, too soon, or you risk altitude sickness. At the first sign of any illness like headache or nausea, just head down the mountain. Going down a couple thousand feet is all you need to quickly recover.

It has recently become exceedingly popular to bicycle down the Haleakala Highway. The road is quite narrow, so watch out for groups of bicycles. If you'd like to try this beautiful ride, there are plenty of companies offering the trip.

Ask lots of questions before settling on a company. Do they pick you up? That can be a mixed blessing if you have to get up at 3:00 a.m. and then get hauled around for hours for other pickups. You might save money and time by choosing a tour that has you get yourself to the cycle home base. Be sure to ask what time they actually begin biking, how large is the group, and when and where you will eat.

On the way, at about 3,000' you will be in the area called "upcountry" where you can ride horses and check out an entirely different side of Maui. This is ranch country where they still raise

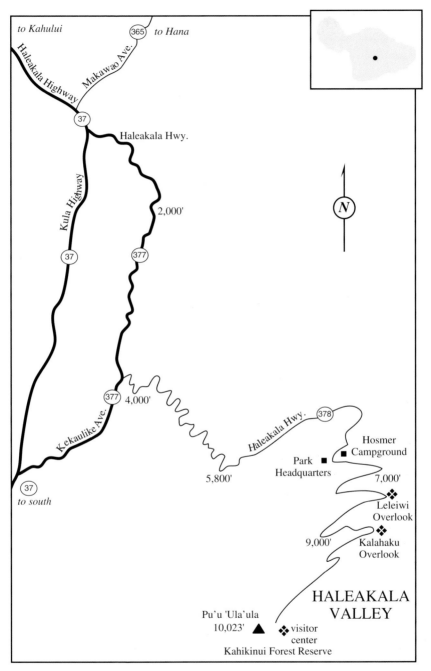

to Kahului (365) to Hana

Haleakala Highway

Makawao Ave.

(37)

Haleakala Hwy.

Kula Highway

2,000'

(37) (377)

N

(377) 4,000'

Kekaulike Ave.

Haleakala Hwy. (378)

Hosmer
Campground

Park
Headquarters

5,800' 7,000'

(37)
to south

❖
Leleiwi
Overlook

❖
9,000' Kalahaku
Overlook

HALEAKALA
VALLEY

Pu'u 'Ula'ula
10,023' ▲ ❖ visitor
center
Kahikinui Forest Reserve

excellent beef. It's a chance to see the real working old west – Maui
style. Hawai'ian paniolos learned their ranch skills directly from
Mexico even before the cowboys of what we consider the American
west. Hawai'i wasn't a state back then, but it was a lot further west.

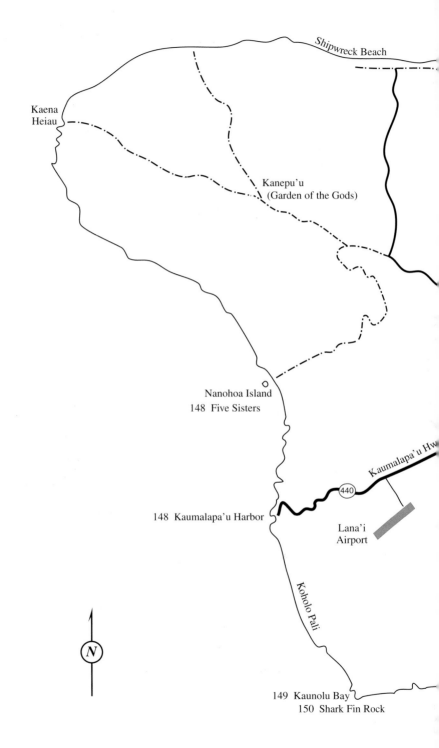

Shipwreck Beach

Kaena
Heiau

Kanepu'u
(Garden of the Gods)

Nanohoa Island
148 Five Sisters

Kaumalapa'u Hwy

440

148 Kaumalapa'u Harbor

Lana'i
Airport

Koholo Pali

N

149 Kaunolu Bay
150 Shark Fin Rock

140

Lana'i Snorkeling Site Index

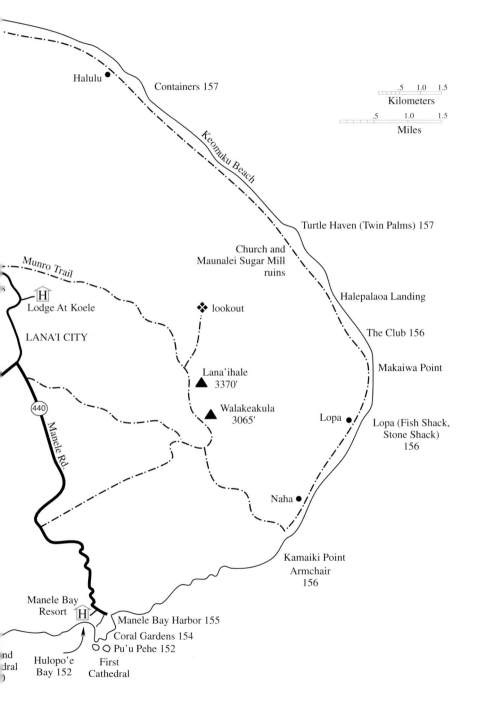

Halulu ●

Containers 157

Keomuku Beach

.5   1.0   1.5
Kilometers

.5   1.0   1.5
Miles

Turtle Haven (Twin Palms) 157

Church and
Maunalei Sugar Mill
ruins

Halepalaoa Landing

Munro Trail

H
Lodge At Koele

❖ lookout

The Club 156

LANA'I CITY

Makaiwa Point

Lana'ihale
▲ 3370'

440

Walakeakula
▲ 3065'

Lopa ●

Lopa (Fish Shack,
Stone Shack)
156

Manele Rd.

Naha ●

Kamaiki Point
Armchair
156

Manele Bay
Resort H

Manele Bay Harbor 155

Coral Gardens 154

◗ ◖ Pu'u Pehe 152

nd
dral

Hulopo'e
Bay 152

First
Cathedral

Lana'i Snorkeling Sites at a Glance

	SNORKELING	ENTRY	SANDY BEACH	RESTROOM	SHOWERS	PICNIC AREA	SCENIC	SHADE
Nanohoa Island	B	1					•	
Kaumalapa'u Harbor	B	1-2						
Kaunolu Bay	A	1					•	
Shark Fin Rock	A	1					•	
Cathedrals	A	1					•	
Hulopo'e Bay	A	1-2	•	•	•	•	•	•
Pu'u Pehe Cove	A	1-2	•				•	
Coral Gardens	A	1-2					•	
Manele Bay	A	2		•	•	•	•	•
Armchair	A	1	•				•	•
Lopa	A	1	•				•	•
Club Lana'i	A	1	•				•	•
Turtle Haven	A	1	•				•	•
Containers	A	1	•				•	•

Lana'i

For that one extra-special snorkeling experience, consider a trip to Lana'i, where beautiful Hulopo'e Bay awaits. A day trip from Lahaina to Lana'i on the Expeditions ferry takes you within five minutes of this famous beach as well as several excellent smaller snorkeling sites.

If your time and budget allow, stay overnight at either of the two big resorts or the one small hotel in Lana'i City.

Numerous excursions offer their own unique trips to Lana'i (for reviews, see excursions from Maui, page 122). We've included our review of the ferry along with hotel information in case you'd like to visit, or better yet, stay awhile. From West Maui, the ferry is usually faster and more convenient than flying. Cars and jeeps can be rented in Lana'i City.

Car Rentals   808-565-7227

Expeditions

Ferry service from Maui to Lana'i departs from Lahaina Harbor, in front of the Pioneer Inn, and arrives at the harbor at Manele Bay 45 minutes later. The cost is $50 round trip for an adult, $40 for children 2-11. This is one of the best deals on Maui for $50.

Five trips go in each direction, each and every day. The ships are obviously designed to be very seaworthy, and few trips are cancelled due to weather. Departures from Lahaina at 6:45 a.m., 9:15 a.m., 12:45 p.m., 3:15 p.m., and 5:45 p.m. Returns from Lana'i at 8:00 a.m., 10:30 a.m., 2:00 p.m., 4:30 p.m., and 6:45 p.m. Reservations are advised if you want a sure seat and they ask that you board 15 minutes early. They do leave right on time, so don't arrive a minute late. Call to be sure departure times haven't changed.

Expeditions I is a 40-foot ship, holding 36 passengers, while Expeditions II is 50 feet, seating 64. It's a smooth, quiet ride with

reef squid

plenty of comfortable, padded seats inside. They serve coffee on the first departure, so even the groggy, caffeine-addicted can enjoy the sunrise. On the late ferry back to Maui, sit on the front deck for a romantic view of the lights of Lahaina.

Packages are available through Expeditions. They can include a car (about $100 per day), golfing ($150) and/or overnight stays on Lana'i at either the Lodge at Koele or the Manele Bay Resort (upwards of $350 per night). Everything on Lana'i makes Maui look like a bargain – except for the wonderful beaches, which are still free.

Expeditions   808-661-3756   P. O. Box 10, HI 96767

Manele Bay Resort

There is only one waterfront hotel in Lana'i and it is exquisite. Spread out on a small hill overlooking a large beach, the Manele Bay Resort has a casual elegance. A championship golf course wraps around in back, providing greenery amid the arid hillside. Rooms are large and very comfortable. The hotel sprawls gracefully on several levels, and it's fun to wander into courtyard gardens with helpful labels for identifying the exotic selection of tropical plants. The feeling is peaceful, quiet and subdued.

The staff is always friendly and they will go out of the way to see that guests have whatever help they need. Breakfast in the room arrives at precisely the time ordered and provides an ample treat to savor on the patio.

The outlying rooms require a hike to the pool, then another hike down the hill to the beach. However, shuttles are always waiting in front of the lobby to offer transportation to the beach or elsewhere on Lana'i.

Decor is tastefully understated, dramatic yet informal, with lots of antique art objects collected from China. The cuisine has received outstanding reviews. And pods of spinner dolphins cruise the snorkeling beach.

Manele Bay Resort provides luxurious relaxation at premium prices, $350 and up for a night. Several of the best snorkeling spots on Lana'i are within walking distance. And there's certainly enough to keep you busy for a week. Few snorkelers would complain if heaven looked and worked just like the Manele Bay Resort.

800-321-4666   www.lanai-resorts.com
808-565-3800
808-565-3868 fax

The Lodge at Koele

For those who can stand being away from the beach, the stately Lodge at Koele provides a cool, green setting among Norfolk Island Pines. Up here in the hills, scenery, service and food are soothing and delightful. The Lodge also has an adjacent garden, pool, pond and golf course. Riding stables are nearby. Shuttles to the beach are always available. This unique resort is worth a visit even if you don't plan to stay. The lobby looks like a casual museum, with fine Asian antiques everywhere.

Each afternoon at four they set out a serve-yourself classic British tea with scones and much more for guests from The Lodge or the Manele Bay Resort. Of course, guests here can also take the shuttle down to the beach, leaving each half hour. Rates start at around $350 per night.

The Lodge at Koele   (800) 321-4666

Disposable Underwater Cameras

Cheap, widely available, even stocked on some excursions, and fun to use. Keep your expectations realistic and you won't end up disappointed, although you won't get pictures like you see in National Geographic. The professionals who get all those great shots use camera setups worth $10,000 and more. They also have assistants underwater to hold the lights and spare cameras. Their books start to look like bargains compared with trying to get these pictures by yourself. Check out the great selection of marine life books in Maui bookstores.

Still, it's fun to try for that cute shot of your sweetie in a bikini, clowning with the fish. If you're lucky, you'll actually have identifiable fish in a few shots. The cameras won't focus closer than about four feet, so the fish will look much smaller than you remember them. These cameras work best when it's sunny with good visibility and the subject fish as close as the camera allows.

They do work OK above the water too, so make a great knock-around camera to haul around wet or dry without paranoia about theft, saltwater or damage. Try a picture of the beautiful hills of Maui as you float in the waters of 'Ahihi Bay.

On Your Own

In Lana'i, just a five-minute walk from the harbor brings you to some of the best snorkeling and swimming at broad and beautiful Hulopo'e Bay. Showers, restrooms, shade and a beautiful wide sand beach await you. The Manele Bay Resort is steps away, if you require more (especially gourmet dining).

Come early, stay late and try several different snorkeling spots within easy walking distance. The full day trip gives you ample time to check out the Manele Bay Resort before walking over to the harbor. You'll have time for a drink or meal and a walk around this lovely hotel. No car is needed if you just want to snorkel or swim.

If you are eager to see it all, take a whirlwind car tour. Try the Munro Trail north of Lana'i City if you rent a jeep and it hasn't just rained. You'll want to catch the first ferry of the day. Bring a picnic lunch, try the local fare in Lana'i City or splurge at the big resorts – both resorts have food the critics rave about. You can't see everything in one day, but you can have a great time and will want to return.

Lana'i has a shortage of water so uses reclaimed water for both golf courses and landscaping; often even showers. Be aware that you shouldn't drink shower water. Hulopo'e and Manele Bay provide drinking water as well in large coolers spread along the beach. Excursions all bring their own water, other drinks and paper cups as well. With all the sun, you'll need plenty of fluids, especially if you're soaking up the sun on the ship while in transit.

We've arranged these Lana'i sites in counter-clockwise order following the coast. We list no sites along the wave-pounded, exposed northern shore, so begin on the far western side of Lana'i.

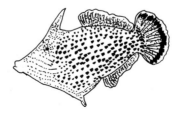

fantail filefish

147

Nanohoa Island (Five Sisters)

Five Sisters got its name from the five tall pinnacles located just south of the shore. One of the sisters fell during Hurricane Ewa in 1982. This is a gorgeous location on Lana'i's far western shore, but has relatively small amounts of coral and fish. This is a perfect place to anchor for lunch and well worth the trip to see this lovely coast.

GETTING THERE   The only practical access here is by boat. It can be reached by the faster boats heading out from Lahaina. The zodiac-type boats have no problem circling Lana'i when weather is cooperative and you've chosen the longer trip (see map, page 140).

Kaumalapa'u Harbor

Kaumalapa'u Harbor (often called Barge Harbor) is an unlikely-looking snorkeling site. It has fine snorkeling, however, and offers some unusual fish including schools of pyramid butterflyfish. Don't go on a Thursday – the only day this big harbor is in full operation.

You'll find a small reef with fairly easy entry, clear water and lots to see. You do need to enter from rocks, slowly and carefully. Parking and crowds are certainly no problem here. Small waves break over the shallow reef in the center, making it look rougher than it really is. Swimming around the outside of the reef is usually easy and quite safe, but use care if swimming directly over such a shallow reef. Experts can manage it when the tide is high enough.

GETTING THERE   From Lana'i City, take Highway 440 west to the harbor. Since Lana'i has few roads, it's easy to find (see map, page 149). Use the harbor parking lot and snorkel on the right side where you can see the reef from the lot. It's right next to shore. Enter to the left of the reef from the rocks and swim entirely around it if you wish.

spotted boxfish

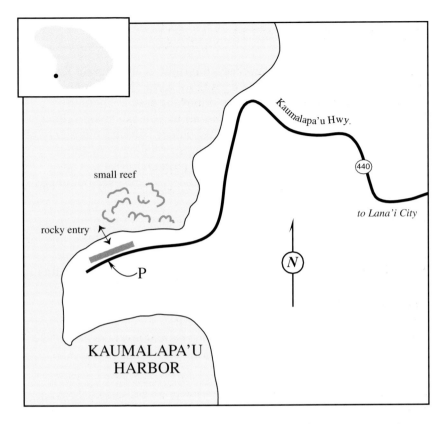

small reef

rocky entry

P

KAUMALAPA'U
HARBOR

Kaumalapa'u Hwy.

440

to Lana'i City

N

Kaunolu Bay

This usually calm, sheltered bay near the lighthouse in the southwest offers clear water with patches of reef and coral habitat. Most Lana'i sites are more exposed to open ocean, so Kaunolu Bay has an advantage when other sites are too choppy. There's a sandy bottom and mooring balls for several boats. Plenty of reef fish make this an excellent choice. Since it's right next to Shark Fin Rock, boats can easily take you to both.

GETTING THERE   There's no way you will be able to get to Kaunolu Point from the land. Fast excursions from Lahaina (see chapter about excursions) can zip over here for a day trip – especially the zodiac-type boats. These are the highest cliffs in Lana'i, so you won't find any kind of road down to the water.

Shark Fin Rock

This is a great snorkel and dive location right near Kaunolu Point. A very dramatic location, this site derives its name from a large rock in the shape of a shark's fin – sticking out of the water. There are numerous little coves to explore for as far as you can swim. The coral isn't spectacular here (more of a boulder habitat), but plenty of fish hang out near the rocks. Most of the snorkeling is in about 10-20'-deep water near shore with some protection from swells. Watch carefully along the boulders because you may see octopuses and eels here.

When calm enough, do snorkel all the way around Shark Fin Rock because the back provides a wonderful view of the deep drop-off where we saw schools of pyramid butterflyfish – rarely seen in Maui's shallower water. The floor drops off quickly here providing a habitat for somewhat different fish and the dark blue water is delightful.

GETTING THERE   Once again, this site can't be reached from land. Only the faster boats will attempt to come this far from Lahaina (see map, page 140).

Cathedrals

Cathedrals sites are located along the cliffs of the southern shore of Lana'i. Trilogy runs a small catamaran as an optional day trip for their Lana'i excursion clients, and it's delightful. Scuba is often offered here as well. You will find other excursions from Maui that visit Cathedrals (see Excursions, page 122). A shelf of coral extends out from the cliffs at just the right height for snorkelers. You will probably be the only group of snorkelers in sight. Of course, if you are feeling brave and indestructible, you could jump in from the high cliffs as ancient Hawai'ians did. Getting out would be another matter!

GETTING THERE   This large site is for excursions only. Trilogy sometimes heads here from Manele Bay, Navatek from Lahaina, Ultimate Rafting from Lahaina, and several of the newer, faster boats. When south swells roll in, all are likely to head elsewhere because they don't you washing up on the base of the cliff.

150

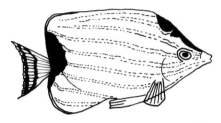

bluestripe butterflyfish

Hulopo'e Bay

This large, beautiful bay in front of the Manele Bay Resort is famous for good reasons. The lovely wide sand beach has showers, restrooms, drinking water, grass, and shade. Limited camping is allowed here, with a permit that must be obtained in Maui. This is one of the most dramatic beachside camping sites in Hawai'i.

When calm, you can snorkel anywhere, but don't miss the row of coral peninsulas jutting out like underwater ship piers over on the left all the way to the point. Cruise up the dramatic mini-canyons between them. We have seen big spiny lobster here in the daytime, as well as pelagic fish, parrotfish, raccoon butterflyfish, boxfish, many wrasses, eels and quite often pods of spinner dolphins (as many as two hundred at once).

If surf is high (especially with south swell), don't get caught between the waves and coral or rocks. We saw a variety of weather in a few days – from calm as glass throughout the bay to breakers. Keep in mind that all of the Lana'i snorkeling sites face open ocean, so conditions vary depending on which way the swells are rolling.

Even if swell is breaking, good swimmers can usually go beyond, since the coral extends beyond the bay. Stay within the bay to avoid any currents. The water is usually wonderfully clear. A good part of the bay is about 10-20 feet deep. On the far left you'll see stairs coming down from the hill to tidepools, which are fun for kids. Do check the tide and surf conditions carefully first.

GETTING THERE   From the Manele Bay Hotel, follow the path down to the beach and continue to the far left for the best snorkeling. (see map, page 153). From the Manele Harbor it's a five-minute walk. Head out the exit road and take the first left.

Pu'u Pehe Cove

Pu'u Pehe Cove is also called Shark Cove. If you don't mind climbing down a twenty-foot cliff, which does have a crude trail, and is actually much easier than it looks, this bay has a pretty sandy beach and excellent snorkeling. No crowds down on this beach! Pu'u Pehe Cove and adjacent Coral Gardens are our favorite shore-entry sites on Lana'i. Entry is easy from the sandy beach when calm. Snorkel to the left between the rocks, then continue as far as you like around the various rocks out to sea, unless you encounter currents near the far point. As always, waves can vary in size and come from different

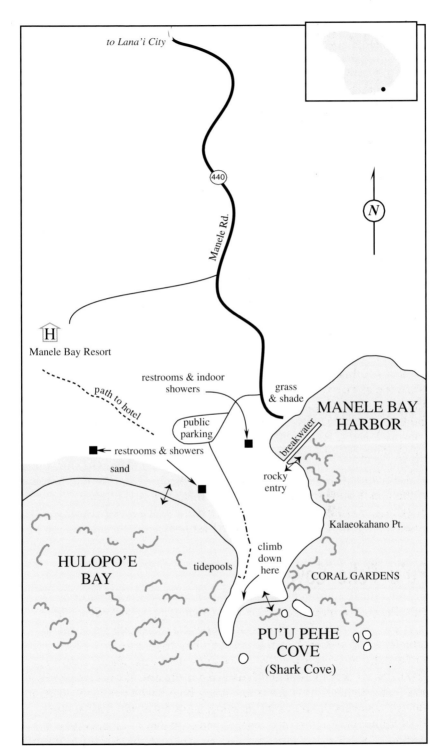

to Lana'i City

440

Manele Rd.

N

H

Manele Bay Resort

path to hotel

restrooms & indoor showers

grass & shade

MANELE BAY HARBOR

breakwater

public parking

restrooms & showers

sand

rocky entry

Kalaeokahano Pt.

climb down here

HULOPO'E BAY

tidepools

CORAL GARDENS

PU'U PEHE COVE

(Shark Cove)

153

directions, so conditions are quite changeable from day to day. Since this beach is fairly isolated in spite of being so close to a big hotel, don't snorkel here unless you feel sure that you can easily handle the ocean conditions. Of course, never snorkel alone at an isolated site like this. When the sea is calm, snorkel out through the shallow channel to the left and wander through Coral Gardens. We've seen plenty of fish, eels, and even an octopus up close.

When swells are too large, entry becomes dangerous in spite of the sandy beach, so don't try this one if you have doubts. Anyway, the water won't be very clear when waves are up.

GETTING THERE   From Hulopo'e Bay, walk out on the dirt road toward the far left point, past the stairs to the tidepools (see map, page 153). Be sure to wear tennis shoes or reef shoes, hat and sunglasses since there's no shade. At the point we've marked on the map you'll find the only place to climb down the cliff on the far side. It helps if one person climbs down first and another passes them the gear. It's not as difficult as it looks, providing you go slowly and hold on carefully. There are no facilities here and little shade, but it's dramatic and worthwhile for . swimmers and snorkelers. Serious snorkelers won't want to miss this one. All facilities are available at nearby Hulopo'e Beach.

Coral Gardens

Just to the northeast of Pu'u Pehe, you can snorkel along the coast all the way to Manele Harbor if it happens to be calm. Go slow and check to see if there's any current before heading out too far. You'll find some good snorkeling along the rocky coast and patches of coral a bit further from shore. While there isn't a lot of coral, you'll usually find plenty of fish. This isn't for beginners because it can be quite choppy with a current. Besides, there won't be anyone around to help out if you get in trouble.

GETTING THERE   From the Manele Bay Hotel, follow our instructions to Pu'u Pehe (see map, page 153). As you enter the water make a left turn and snorkel between the rocks, then continue along the coast on your left.

From the Manele Harbor, enter at the spot we have marked just south of the main Manele Harbor (see map, page 153). If conditions are calm enough, continue south along the coast – perhaps even ending up at Pu'u Pehe.

Manele Bay (The Harbor)

This appears at first glance to be an unlikely-looking place to snorkel. However, it has an excellent assortment of fish and coral for such a small site. Simply step off the boat or ferry, snorkel in the little cove outside the breakwater, where you're away from harbor boat traffic. When calm, you can continue out toward the point or further out from the breakwater, where excursions often bring their snorkelers.

There's a grassy park next to the harbor with restrooms, indoor showers, drinking water, picnic tables and shade – everything except a beach. You could have a fine day trip right here. You'll probably have the little cove to yourself. Explore along the breakwater, and weave in and out among the coral heads towards the point. In very calm weather, an expert snorkeler can swim all the way to Hulopo'e Bay. Caution – it's a very long swim!

In the murky waters of the harbor itself, baby hammerhead sharks are sometimes seen. We wouldn't recommend snorkeling there, on the remote chance that a grumpy parent might be around to bump into. Harbors aren't great for snorkeling anyway since boat traffic is dangerous.

GETTING THERE   From the the Manele Harbor dock, turn toward the tiny cove on the south side of the small breakwater (see map, page 153). There's no beach, and entry is a bit tricky from the rocks at the north corner of the cove. See the map. Wear shoes even though it's a short distance because the rocks can be slippery, sharp and sometimes hot. Entry is from the rocks, so take great care not to slip. You'll wonder why you're here until you duck your head underwater. If you encounter a current or large swells, stay within this sheltered area. If calm, you can snorkel out and along the coast to the right. Beginners should not try this entry, but can snorkel the area from a boat. Although often choppy, there lots to see, so experienced snorkelers are likely to love it.

Alternatively, you can enter the water from the dock and swim to the right around the breakwater – watching out for boat traffic and looking for those baby sharks at the same time.

Armchair (Kamaiki Point)

Armchair has a pinnacle about 75 yards offshore, where you will find fish and coral near the top. This is a popular dive site. Snorkelers need help finding the spot, so it's best to arrive by boat. It isn't always a safe place to snorkel since swells and currents can be a problem at this exposed southeastern site.

GETTING THERE   Though possible by land, access is better by boat with a captain to show you where it is. Besides, waves are often rolling in along the whole eastern side of Lana'i. The snorkeling area is well beyond the waves, but can be choppy enough to make it better for diving than snorkeling. While this site can be calmer than those further north, it's still vulnerable to open ocean conditions. You'll also want to snorkel here only when visibility is good.

Lopa (Stone Shack)

This extensive snorkeling site (also called Stone Shack or Fish Shack) is at the southern end of Lana'i's seven-mile long reef. You can wander up and down this broad reef, always staying away from the waves breaking against the shore. The reef extends to the shore, but boats anchor well beyond the waves. Most of this reef is ten to twenty feet beneath the surface, so it helps to have good visibility.

Some patches of reef may seem to have few fish, but keep snorkeling and you're bound to come across big groups of fish as well as plenty of turtles. This is usually the calmest spot along Lana'i's long eastern reef. Summer swells can ruin the visibility.

GETTING THERE   This site is best accessed by day-trip boat. They can place you well beyond any danger from waves hitting the shore. The captain can assess the best conditions and visibility along this extensive reef. Shore access is possible, but should be left to experienced local snorkelers because it involves a swim over coral and through waves (see map, page 141).

The Club

This section of Lana'i's largest reef is directly in front of a privately-owned eight-acre chunk of land where Club Lana'i used to take its excursions. The future of the land is unsure, but the reef in front is still in good condition. Like Stone Shack to the south, The Club (also called Club Lana'i or Coral Gardens) offers broad reef extending in both directions and is a popular excursion destination. Most of the reef is about 10-20 feet deep. While the fish aren't concentrated in one spot, you can wander through a broad area and see plenty of coral, fish and turtles.

GETTING THERE   This is a popular site with excursions from Maui because there's plenty to see and they can easily find sandy areas to anchor without damaging the coral. Entry from land is not available at the moment and would be hazardous due to the waves over coral close to shore. There is a nice, sandy beach with very shallow water – perfect for small children if and when it's available again.

Turtle Haven (Twin Palms)

Heading north from Club Lana'i along the long reef you'll find Turtle Haven (often called Twin Palms). While the tall palms on the beach mark this site, there are several other pairs of palms along this coast so you probably wouldn't find it on your own. This site is within the seven-mile long reef and has a natural bowl in the coral where turtles like to hang out. With them will be tangs who like to eat algae off the turtles' shells. The coral here is beautiful and has channels of sand running perpendicular to shore.

GETTING THERE   Beach access is only available to experienced locals on this remote northeastern coast of Lana'i. Boats from Lahaina make the trip when conditions are good. When swells from the north kick in, they're likely to go further south for calm conditions.

Containers

This northernmost site on the seven-mile long reef is named for the shipping container seen on the beach. The coral here is unusually beautiful. The northeast location means relatively few days of calm seas. When the trade winds start to blow from the northeast (75% of the time), head south to snorkel.

GETTING THERE   Too remote for beach access, you'll have to come by boat on one of the excursions out of Lahaina. Only the faster boats are likely to come this far and only with good conditions, so this isn't a site you can count on. Trust your captain to decide if it's a good choice.

Marine Life

The coral reef supports tremendous diversity in a small space. On a healthy reef, you've never seen everything, because of the boggling variety of species, as well as changes from day to day and changes from day to night. The reef functions much like the oasis in the desert providing food (more abundant than the open ocean) and shelter from predators. Only the wild rain forests can compare with the reef in complexity.

In Hawai'i the reef coral itself is less spectacular than in warmer waters of the world. This is counterbalanced by the colorful and abundant fish, which provide quite a show.

There are excellent color fish identification cards available in bookstores and dive shops. We particularly like the ones published by Natural World Press. There are also many good marine life books that give far more detailed descriptions of each creature than we attempt in these brief notes.

OCTOPUS

Some varieties of octopuses hide during the day; others will hunt for food then. They eat shrimp, fish, crabs, and mollusks – you should eat so well! Octopuses have strong "beaks" and can bite humans, so it's safer to not handle them.

Being mollusks without shells, they must rely on speed, cunning and camouflage to escape danger. Octopuses are capable of imitating a flashing sign, or changing their color and texture to match their surroundings in an instant. This makes them very hard to spot, even when they're hiding in plain sight – usually on the bottom or on rocks. They also squirt an ink to confuse predators or prey. They live about two years.

Just because you haven't seen one doesn't mean they aren't there. Go slow and watch carefully for the "rock" that moves.

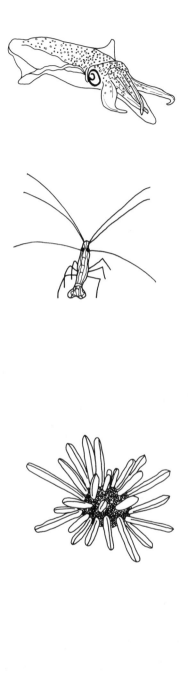

REEF SQUID

These graceful, iridescent creatures hang around reef areas, often forming a single long line. All eyes will follow you easily since they have 360 degree vision. They can capture surprisingly large fish with their tentacles.

SHRIMP

In all kinds, colors, and sizes, they like to hide in rocks and coral – often living symbiotically with the coral. They are difficult to spot during the daytime, but at night you will notice lots of tiny pairs of eyes reflected in the flashlight beam. Most are fairly small and well-disguised.

Some examples include: the harlequin shrimp (brightly colored) that eat sea stars, the banded coral shrimp (found all over the world), and numerous tiny shrimp that you won't see without magnification.

SEA URCHINS

Concealed tube feet allow urchins to move around in their hunt for algae. The collector urchin has pebbles and bits of coral attached for camouflage. These urchins are quite common in Hawai'i, and have no spines.

Beware of purple-black urchins with long spines. These are common in shallow water at certain beaches. It's not the long spines that get you, it's the ones beneath. The bright red pencil sea urchin is common and easy to spot. Although large, its spines aren't sharp enough to be a problem for people.

CRINOIDS

These animals seen on top of the rocks or coral can easily be mistaken for plants. They are sometimes called "feather stars" and are delicate and beautiful plankton feeders.

SEA STARS

Abundant, in many colors and styles. The crown of thorns sea star, which can be such a devastator of coral reefs, is found in Hawai'i, but not in large numbers like the South Pacific. Sea stars firmly grasp their prey with strong suction cups, and then eat at leisure.

RAYS

Manta rays (large plankton-eaters) use two flaps to guide plankton into their huge efficient mouths. Mantas often grow to be two meters from wing-tip to wing-tip, and can weigh 300 pounds. They can't sting, but are large enough to bump hard.

Mantas feed at night by doing forward rolls in the water with mouths wide open. Lights will attract plankton which appeal to the manta rays. Dive boats in favored locations can easily attract them with their bright lights making the night trips quite exciting.

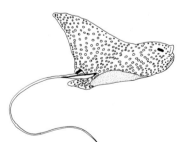

Another beautiful ray, the spotted eagle ray, can sometimes be seen cruising the bottom for food and can grow to be seven feet across. They have a dark back with lots of small white dots and an extremely long tail. Their fins function more like wings to enable them to "fly" along rather than swimming.

Common sting rays prefer the sandy bottom and stay in calm, shallow, warmer water.

EELS

Many types of moray eels abound among the reefs of Maui. They can easily grow up to two meters long.

Varieties of moray found in Hawai'i include whitemouth, snowflake, zebra (black and white stripes), wavy-lined, mottled, and dragon moray (often reddish-brown with distinct white spots of differing sizes).

Morays prefer to hide in holes during the day. If out cruising, they often find a nearby hole when spotting a snorkeler. When they stick out their heads and breathe, their teeth are most impressive.

Eels generally have no interest in eating snorkelers, other than very annoying ones, while they are quite happy and able to swallow a fairly large fish.

TRUMPETFISH

These long, skinny fish can change color, often bright yellow or light green – and will change right in front of your eyes. They sometimes hang upright to blend with their environment, lying in wait to suck in their prey. Sometimes they shadow another fish to sneak up on prey – even at a cleaning station.

They do eat during the day, which is unusual for fish-eaters, who usually eat at dawn or dusk. Trumpetfish are quite common in Hawai'i and often seen alone. Some grow to more than one meter long.

NEEDLEFISH

These pointed, common silvery-blue fish like swimming very near the surface, usually in schools – occasionally leaping from the water. All types of needlefish are long and skinny as their name implies, and grow to as much as 1-2 feet long. Color and markings vary, but the long narrow shape is distinctive and hard to mistake. They're usually bluish on top, and translucent below for camouflage.

BUTTERFLYFISH

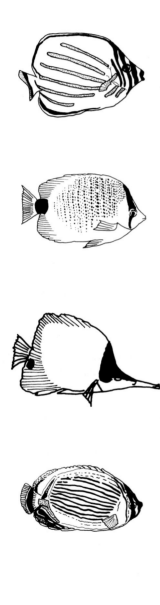

Butterflyfish are beautiful, colorful, abundant and varied in Hawai'i. They have incredible coloration, typically bright yellow, white, orange, black, and sometimes a little blue. They hang out near coral, eating algae, sponges, tube worms and coral polyps. No one really understands the purpose of their beautiful colors, but many have speculated. Perhaps they serve territorial needs.

Juveniles are often distinctly different in coloring. Bizarre patterns may confuse predators – especially since they can pivot fast. Bars may help some hide, while stripes are seen more in faster fish. Black lines across the eyes and spots near the tail also confuse predators.

Butterflyfish are often seen in pairs remaining together for up to three years. They're delightful to watch. Hovering and turning are more important to them than speed since they stay near shelter of the reef and catch a quick meal – like a tube worm.

The ones you are most likely to see in Hawai'i include: raccoon (reminding you of the face of the animal), ornate (with bright orange lines making it easy to spot), threadfin (another large, beautiful one), saddleback, lemon (very tiny), bluestripe (a beautiful one found only in Hawai'i), fourspot, milletseed, oval, teardrop, and forceps (also called long nose). The lined butterflyfish is the largest variety found in Hawai'i.

Many butterflyfish have black spots near the tail – perhaps to confuse a predator about which way they're headed. Watch and they may confuse you.

PARROTFISH

Among the most dramatically colored fish on the reef, male parrotfish are blue, green, turquoise, yellow, lavender, and/or orange with endless variations of these colors. Females tend to be reddish brown. No two are alike. Parrotfish are very beautiful, with artistic, abstract markings.

These fish change colors at different times in their lives and can also change sex as needed. They can be quite large (up to one meter).

Patient grazers, they spend countless hours scraping algae from dead coral with their large, beak-like teeth, and create tons of white sand in the process. Most prefer to zoom away from snorkelers, but you'll see them passing gracefully by and will hear them crunching away at the coral.

TRIGGERFISH

Fond of sea urchins as a main course, triggerfish graze during the day on algae, worms and other small items.

Varieties include the Picasso (wildly colorful – not too many at each beach, but worth watching for), reef (the Hawai'ian state fish), pinktail (easy to identify with its black body, white fins and pink tail), black (common, distinctive white lines between body and fins). The checkerboard triggerfish has a pink tail, yellow-edged fins, and blue stripes on its face. All triggerfish are very beautiful and fascinating to watch.

FILEFISH

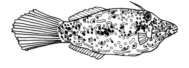

The scrawled filefish has blue scribbles and brown dots over its olive green body. Quite large, up to one meter, often in pairs, but seen occasionally in groups.

A filefish will often turn its body flat to your view, and raise its top spine in order to impress you. This lets you have a great close-up view – a perfect photo opportunity.

The brown filefish (endemic) is much smaller, with lines on its head and white spots on its brown body. The fantail filefish (also endemic and small) has a distinct orange tail and lots of black spots over a light body. Filefish will sometimes change color patterns rapidly for camouflage.

SURGEONFISH

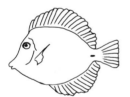

Razor-sharp fin-like spines on each side of the tail are the hallmark of this fish, quite common in Hawai'i. These spines provide excellent defense, but aren't needed to fend off tourists since surgeonfish can easily swim away.

Varieties includes the orangeband surgeonfish (with distinctive long, bright orange marks on the side), as well as the Achilles tang (also called naso tang), which has bright orange spots surrounding the spines near the orange tail. The yellow tang is completely yellow and smaller. The sailfin tang has dramatic vertical markings. It's less common, but easy to identify.

WRASSES

Wrasses are amazingly bright and multicolored fish. Some very small ones set themselves up for business and operate a cleaning station, where they clean much larger fish without having to worry about becoming dinner. They eat parasites, and provide an improbable reef service in the process. Perhaps their bright colors serve as neon signs to advertise their services Hang out near their cleaning stations for excellent fish viewing. In Hawai'i, the cleaner wrasse is bright yellow, purple and black.

Other wrasses are large including the dazzling yellowtail (up to 15 inches), which has a red body covered with glowing blue spots, a few stripes, and a bright yellow tail.

Another large wrasse, the saddleback, is endemic to Hawai'i. It is bright blue, with green and orange markings. Wrasses are closely related to parrotfish. Like parrotfish, they can change colors and sex.

SCORPIONFISH

This improbable-looking fish is very colorful, with feather-like multicolor spines. Beware of their poisonous spines, though! Don't even think about touching a scorpionfish, and try to avoid accidentally stepping on one.

This varied group of exotic fish includes the bright red Hawai'ian turkeyfish, sometimes called a lionfish.

Others are so well-camouflaged that they are hard to see. They just lurk on the bottom blending in well with the sand and coral. If you see one, count yourself lucky.

PUFFERFISH

Pufferfish (and the related trunkfish) swim slowly, so need more protection. Some can blow up like balloons when threatened.

Two kinds are common in sheltered areas: porcupine (displaying spines when inflated), and spotted trunkfish and boxfish (often brown or black with lots of white dots). They tend to prefer to escape under the coral, although some seem unafraid of snorkelers.

SHARKS

Although sharks have quite a reputation for teeth rather than brains, they are unquestionably survivors, having been around for about 300 million years.

This is an extremely successful species with keen hearing, smell, sight and ability to detect electrical signals through the water. They swim with a side-to-side motion, which does not make them speedy by ocean standards.

When snorkeling you are unlikely to spot any shark except the reef or white-tipped lazing around shallow water. Plenty of larger species pass by Hawai'i, but tend to prefer the deeper waters in the channels.

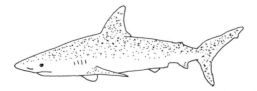

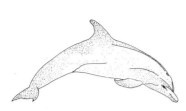

DOLPHINS

Spinner dolphins are frequently seen in large schools (about 200). They swim as small family groups within these schools, and often swim fast, leaping from the water, spinning in the air. They tend to hang out in certain locations, so you can search them out if you like.

Bottlenose dolphins often approach fast-moving boats, and it is a great thrill to watch them race along just next to the bow of your boat, jumping in and out of the water with grace and easy speed.

Beaked and spotted dolphins are also commonly seen in Hawai'i.

SEA TURTLES

Common at many Maui reefs, though they usually stay away from humans. Some do seem nearly tame – or at least unconcerned about snorkelers.

Sea turtles are often seen in pairs. Larger specimens (often seen at Maluaka and Five Graves) might be more than 100 years old, and tend to be docile and unafraid. You'll often see them resting on the bottom in about ten to twenty feet of water during the day. They will let you swim as close as you like, but if you hover over them, they might be afraid to come up for air.

Do not disturb these graceful creatures, so that they can remain unafraid to swim among snorkelers. In Hawai'i it is against the law to touch or harass these magnificent animals.

WHALES

Humpback whales migrate here to breed in winter, around early-December. Humpbacks come quite close to the coast, where you can watch whole families. They are so large that you can often easily see them spouting and breaching. If you bring binoculars, you can see them well from shore. Their great size never fails to impress, as does their fluid, seemingly effortless graceful movement in the water.

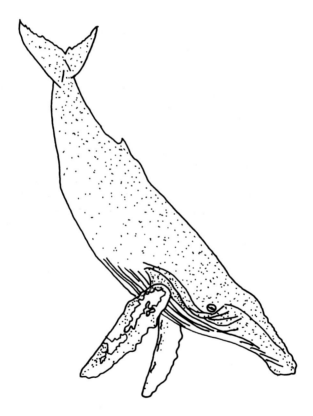

If You Love the Reef

- Show respect for the reef creatures by causing them no harm.

- Avoid touching the coral, as touching kills it.

- Come as a respectful visitor rather than as a predator.

- Leave the many beautiful creatures you find there in peace so that others may enjoy them as you have.

- Allow the fish their usual diet rather than feeding them. Feeding them ultimately destroys their natural balance, and causes their numbers to decline.

- Think of the creatures of the reef as fellow travelers in our life journey and then you may comprehend their magnificence.

- Join our reef easter egg hunt: try to find and dive for at least one piece of trash on every snorkel, and take it away with you. It sharpens your eye, and if enough folks do it, it will be hard to find any. Don't try to clean up the whole world. Just pick up one or two things every time you're out.

- Use sunscreen less, and cover-ups more. Sunscreen dissolves in the water, and is toxic to fish and coral. A lycra body suit or a wetsuit takes care of most of your body better anyway. Save your sunscreen for your sensitive face.

Weather

All islands have a windward side, which is wetter, and a leeward side which is drier. In Hawai'i, the northeast is windward and hence wet, and the southwest is leeward, or kona, and hence drier and sunnier. Waves from afar tend to arrive from the north in winter and from the south in summer, although this pattern changes often.

Hawai'i gets most of its rain in the winter. The most severe storms (called kona), however, come from the south and can even bring hurricanes in the summer. Temperatures tend to be very mild year-round, yet there is variety around Maui on any day of the year. There are days when you could tan in Kihei in the morning, drive up to cold Haleakala later, while rain continues in Hana. Generally summer temperatures are at least five degrees F warmer than winter.

Evaporating moisture from the ocean forms clouds. As the clouds rise over the mountains, they cool, and the condensing moisture becomes rain. The West Maui Mountains receive 400 inches of rain a year, while nearby Lahaina only gets about 30 inches.

Having lost most of their moisture in passing over the mountains, the clouds have little left for the leeward side – so it is in the rain shadow of the mountains. The leeward weather is therefore often sunny. Waikiki, Poipu, Ka'anapali, and Kona are all in rain shadows. On Maui if you get stuck with heavy rains in Hana, just head for Kihei or Wailea to find the sun.

Changeable is the word for Maui's weather – not just between areas, but also rapidly changeable in any given place. The trade winds blow about 90% of the time in the summer and about 50% in the winter. They tend to be stronger in the afternoon.

The following weather notes focus on the leeward or west coasts, since that is where most tourists congregate. The windward or northeastern coasts have much more rain, wind and waves.

Christmas Wrasse

Seasonal Changes

Maui has much milder weather than the continental United States, yet it is has seasons you might call winter, spring and summer. At 20°N Latitude, there are nearly 2 1/2 hours more sun in midsummer than in midwinter, which is 21% more. But the moderating effect of the ocean keeps temperature swings quite moderate.

Winter is the cooler, wetter season. Cooler is a relative term, as the average high temperature in winter falls to a brisk 80° F, as opposed to a summer average high of 88° F. Water temperature in winter falls to around 77° F, and at times, wind, rain and cooler air temperatures can temper your desire to splash around in the water. Winter usually begins in mid-November, with the start of winter storms from the north-northwest. This is the start of the large wave season on the north coast. Winter tails off in mid-March.

Spring really is just the transition from winter to summer, and is marked by the end of winter storms in mid-March. Hours of sunshine go up, especially on the west, leeward side of the island. This can be a very pleasant time of year. Spring transitions into summer in May.

Summer begins in May, as the weather warms, and the rains slacken. Trade winds temper the heat and humidity almost all the time. This is prime sunning and play time. An occasional tropical storm or hurricane can come through, and swells can roll in from the south. The heat softens in October as summer draws to an end.

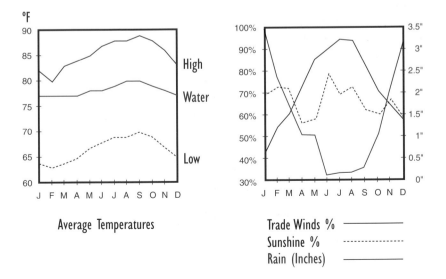

Average Temperatures

Trade Winds %
Sunshine %
Rain (Inches)

Month by Month

JANUARY: This month offers an opportunity for the wettest weather all year. It's also one of the coolest. Large surf can often pound the north and west exposed beaches.

FEBRUARY: Just as cool, the surf continues to hit the north and west exposed beaches, although storms are a bit less frequent.

MARCH: The weather starts to improve with fewer storms, especially on West Maui.

APRIL: Spring arrives early, so warm weather begins during this month.

MAY: Summer is already arriving – especially in Western Maui. This tends to be a trouble-free month.

JUNE: This offers very warm and dry weather with plenty of sun. Fortunately the winds blow nearly every day.

JULY: Much the same as June, except that storms in the South Pacific begin at this time. They hit beaches exposed to the south.

AUGUST: Another warm month, occasional big waves can hit the southern exposed beaches.

SEPTEMBER: This last month of summer can sometimes be the hottest and most humid. Hurricanes rarely strike Maui and Lana'i, but they are most common this month. They usually miss the islands, but bring muggy weather.

OCTOBER: Milder weather begins this month with the start of storms arriving from the north.

NOVEMBER: Sometimes the first real winter storms arrive and they can be somewhat cool.

DECEMBER: This is winter with frequent storms and wind bringing big waves to the exposed northern and western beaches. However, even this month can be clear and warm between storms.

Coolest month:	February
Hottest month:	September
Rainiest month:	January
Driest month:	June
Coolest water:	December-April
Warmest water:	August-September

172

Tides

Tides are very slight in Maui, with the average difference between high and low only 2-3 feet max. It's a good idea to know which way the tide is going because tidal flow does affect the currents. If the tide is going out, you might want to avoid snorkeling in places where water is already shallow or currents tend to sweep out of a bay, often the center, or a gap in the reef (see Understanding waves, page 27). For most of Maui's beaches, this has very little effect.

Water Temperature

On the surface the water in Maui averages a low of about 77° F (25° C) in March to a high of about 80° F (27° C) in September. Sheltered bays can be a bit warmer, while deeper or rough water can be surprisingly cool. Kaua'i (further north) can be even cooler. If you happen to be slender, no longer young, or from a moderate climate, this can seem cooler than you might like – especially if you like to snorkel for hours.

Hurricanes

Summer is hurricane season, but it is also the time when weather is usually excellent. The storms don't last long, but can be terribly destructive. Hurricanes can bring amazingly heavy rain and winds to all the islands. Any of the islands could receive a direct hit. Maui has escaped major damage from hurricanes in recent years.

Tsunamis

Huge waves can be triggered by earthquakes either locally or far across the Pacific. They've hit Hawai'i numerous times, more often from the north. Some very destructive tsunamis have hit and swept over the lowest land. Depending on the exact direction, they can directly hit a valley and really wipe it out and rinse it clean. It is probably better to not be there when this happens, unless you're one great surfer dude. Tsunami waves can be spaced as far as fifteen minutes apart.

Currently there's plenty of warning and authorities prefer to warn of every possible tsunami just to be safe. It doesn't pay to ignore warnings just because the sea appears calm. If a major earthquake strikes while you're visiting, it's a good idea to head rapidly for high ground. Leave bays or valleys which can act to funnel the effects of a large wave.

Geology

To understand what's happening today in Hawai'i, begin by casting your thoughts back about 30 million years. At that time lava was bubbling out in the middle of the Pacific about 20,000' below the ocean surface, due to a volcanic hot spot directly underneath. Molten rock pushing up through the ocean floor formed volcanoes under the sea. Lava built up, layer after layer, until it finally reached the surface to form the first island.

As the volcanoes grew, the weight of these early islands gradually caused them to sink down again, forming atolls. The Pacific Plate drifted northwest, while the hot spot remained stationary. A long string of more than 30 islands were formed, stretching from Midway Island southeast 1600 miles all the way to the Big Island. Another island is already rising in the sea close to the southeast side of the Big Island. Loihi Sea Mount is now just 3000' under the surface, and will probably join the Big Island as it emerges. Lava flowing into the sea from Kilauea has been intermittently building the Big Island daily toward Loihi.

Most of the current above-water mass is now concentrated in eight islands. Kaua'i, about 5 million years old, is the oldest of these, while the Big Island is less than 1 million years old. As these islands drift approximately 4 inches northwest each year, the lava conduits to their volcanoes bend until new conduits are formed. Eventually, the next volcano in the chain takes over the job of releasing the unremitting pressure from pools of magma far below. The beautiful Haleakala Crater on Maui is now considered extinct and offers a chance to explore one of the Hawai'ian volcanoes.

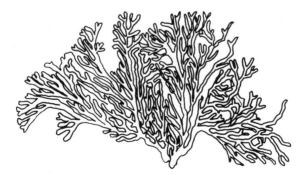

And a Little Natural History, Too

When each underground mountain emerges from the sea, coral larvae begin to establish their new homes on the volcanic rocks around the base. Stony coral is one of the first ocean creatures to reach and become established on a new island.

These larvae travel island by island – originally coming in a very round-about fashion on the currents from the ancient reefs surrounding Indonesia. Once they became established, it was easier for new larvae to reach the next nearby island. The reef begins as a fringe around the island. Each polyp of coral secretes a skeleton of calcium carbonate. Gradually the colony grows large enough to provide a home for other plants and animals.

All of the major Hawai'ian islands now have fringing reefs around much of the shore. The Big Island, still in formation, is not yet fully surrounded by reef. As the islands grow, get heavy and gradually sink, the reef changes as well. The older islands of Kaua'i and O'ahu have very old coral reef deposits on land – remnants of a time when the sea level was higher.

Coral reefs are made up of coral animals and algae growing on top of the dead skeletons of former creatures. In search of sunlight, they continue to grow upward toward the light, as they need to stay within 150 feet of the surface of the sea.

The outside of a reef grows faster than the inner surface, so eventually a lagoon forms between the reef and the land. The reef is then called a barrier reef, limited examples of which can be found in Kaua'i and O'ahu.

Since the currents in Hawai'i come mainly from Japan rather than the warmer south Pacific, they bring less variety of sea life. Larvae need to survive long enough to reach an island and establish themselves before sending out the next generation, so it's helpful to have stepping-stone islands in order to have greater variety. Most will not survive long enough to cross the large open Pacific ocean.

Tahiti, for example, has a much greater variety of coral because of the stepping-stone islands leading all the way from Southeast Asia. Hawai'i, in contrast, is one of the most isolated island groups in the world. It also has somewhat cooler water and less sunlight than Tahiti, making it less hospitable to some species. This isolation has kept all species of plant and animal life rather limited, and also encouraged the evolution of unique species found only in Hawai'i. These unique species are referred to as endemic. They give Hawai'i a special character – both above and below the water. More than 30% of the fish seen here are found nowhere else in the world.

For millions of years the Hawai'ian Islands had no plants or animals in spite of the rich soil, due to their 2000 mile isolation from other large land masses. When plants and animals finally did arrive, they found little competition and a superb climate. The lack of competition meant plants did not require thorns or other protective features. Some plants and animals found such a perfect environment that they thrived. Before man arrived, Hawai'i had no fruits or vegetables. The Polynesians, and later arrivals, changed this environment enormously by their imports and cultivation.

Most of the "exotic" plants that you may think of as quintessentially Hawai'ian were brought by man (mango, papaya, pineapple, orchid, ginger, hibiscus). Koa and ohia (the Hawai'ian state tree), on the other hand, pre-date man's arrival. Ohia is often the first to grow on lava flows and has produced much of the Hawai'ian rain forest.

Unfortunately, most of the rain forest has already been destroyed by animals brought by man (such as cattle and goats) or cleared to provide land for sugar production. Sugar and pineapple production now appear to be on the way out, a casualty of world economics. Tourism has now replaced these crops, but takes its own toll on the fragile islands of Hawai'i.

Moorish idol

Reef Development

Hawai'ian reefs have weathered at least four major changes in the distant past. Many land-based plants and animals also became extinct during these changes and others took their place. Current reefs are composed mostly of shallow water reef coral. They incorporate algae in their structure, and the algae is dependent on photosynthesis.

Different plants and animals live in the varied locations on the reef depending primarily on wave action. Species living on the outer edge of the reef are skilled at surviving strong waves and currents. Lagoon species don't have to endure this, so the lagoon supports more delicate life.

Hawai'i has a number of strikingly different reef habitats – each with its own story to tell. Where the water is rough, cauliflower coral dominates. The more delicate finger coral grows only in the calm lagoon areas. Large boulders are common in the open waters, especially where wave action is heaviest, and they support entirely different creatures. Caves, caverns and old lava tubes are abundant here. Steep drop-offs (like the back of Molokini Island) serve as an upwelling source of plankton-rich water, which attracts many larger creatures to feed. Sandy habitat is found in abundance on Maui. A thriving reef is developing around much of the island.

History

The islands of Hawai'i sat in dramatic isolation for millions of years, slowly softening their volcanic profile, while developing a soft green backdrop. The first people to arrive in the islands were from Polynesia, a culture with a long history of island hopping, dating back to their migration to Polynesia from the Middle East in large double hulled boats.

Fiji was settled by about 3500 B.C., then Samoa and Tonga, and later Tahiti. Hawai'i itself was first settled in waves beginning at least 1200 years ago, probably by voyagers from Tahiti and the Marquesas. They brought everything they needed for a new life here: chickens, dogs, pigs, coconut, bananas. The first landing may have been on the Kona Coast. Many were apparently looking for a form of religious freedom and prospered in this new land. To migrate this far over open ocean required considerable planning and navigational skill, as well as strong motivation.

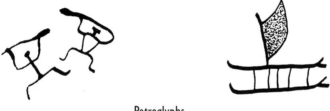

Petroglyphs

Maui

Maui was formed by two volcanoes attached by a low section of land in the center – giving it the nickname "The Valley Island." The oldest volcano, Mauna Kahalawai, created the western section of Maui. Later Haleakala created the eastern part, leaving a huge and fascinating crater, which is now dormant.

Maui remained relatively independent until Chief Kahekili took over Lana'i and Moloka'i – the closest islands. Soon King Kamehameha I from the Big Island forcefully took over Maui as well as most of the other Hawai'ian islands and established his capital in Lahaina. Kamehameha II ruled from 1819 to 1824, but was much weaker and left decisions to Ka'ahumanu (Kamehameha I's favorite wife, who happened to be born in Hana). This was a period of transition away from traditional ways leaving the path clear just as the missionaries and whalers started to arrive. The resulting culture clash was chaos for the Hawai'ians. Although the Kamehameha dynasty was to last 88 years, the times were in flux. The monarchy was over when Queen Lili'uokalani was imprisoned in her own palace – opening Hawai'i to the big business interests. The growers soon arrived with their plantation system and imported laborers (mostly from Japan, China, and the Philippines). They saw profits from fields of sugar cane and pineapple, neither viable crops for Hawai'i these days. Macadamia nuts, sweet onions, coffee, wine, and marijuana have gradually taken the place of the older crops.

Maui has attracted very large numbers of tourists (with over two millions visitors each year) complete with huge hotels, miles of condos, golf courses, competing ships to take you on excursions, and plenty of restaurants, shopping and art galleries. This is quite an industry for an island of little more than 100,000 population.

Lana'i

Lana'i remained unsettled long after the Polynesians arrived on the other Hawai'ian islands, due to its relatively arid climate. Even today the population (2,800) remains quite small for its size. The Mormon Church bought large sections of the island in 1863, hoping to develop a community here. This never happened and title managed to stay with Mr Gibson, who had made the purchase for them.

In 1917 Mr Baldwin purchased most of the island. He sold it for a profit to the Dole Pineapple Company in 1922. Dole proceeded to build a company town to house the workers, many brought from the Philippines – creating the present Lana'i City. Castle and Cooke still owns most of this island and is experimenting with alternative crops, but none on a large scale at this time leaving most of the island untouched. At one time Lana'i was covered with pineapples, and even known as the Pineapple Island, but these days are gone. Pineapple exporting is no longer economic here, since they can be produced cheaper in the South Pacific and elsewhere. Only about 150 acres of pineapple remain for local consumption.

Lana'i is about 98% privately owned. It is legally part of the county that includes Maui and Moloka'i. These three islands would be one if the sea were lower. The other two islands with their high mountains block much of the rain before it reaches Lana'i, so this island doesn't receive enough rainfall on most of the island to support agriculture without irrigation.

Tourism appears to be a better source of income for the present. Manele Bay Resort and The Lodge at Koele are attracting upscale travellers looking for superb accommodations in a serene setting. Each has its own spectacular golf course, which relies on recycled water.

Language

English is now the official language of the islands of Hawai'i – except for the island of Ni'ihau. However, most place names and lots of slang are Hawai'ian, so it's helpful to at least be able to pronounce Hawai'ian enough to be understood. It's a very straight-forward phonetic language – each letter usually pronounced just one way. The long place names aren't nearly so daunting when you've learned the system.

All syllables begin with a consonant that is followed by at least one vowel. When the missionaries attempted to write this spoken language, they used only seven consonants (h,k,l,m,n,p,w) and five vowels (a,e,i,o,u). More recently, in an effort to help outsiders pronounce Hawai'ian, the glottal stop (called an 'okina) has been added – marked by '. For example, in Hawai'i, the ' is used to indicate that each i should be pronounced separately: Ha-wai-i, rather than Ha-waii.

A horizontal line (called a macron) is sometimes placed over vowels to be given a longer duration. Nene, for example, is "Naay-Naay". Unfortunately, our typeface doesn't allow macrons. Each and every letter is pronounced in Hawai'ian, except for a few vowel combinations. However, locals often shorten names a bit, so listen carefully to the way natives pronounce a name. Another addition to the language is a form of pidgin, which served to ease the difficulties of having multiple languages spoken. Laborers were brought in speaking Japanese, Mandarin, Cantonese, Portuguese, English, as well as other languages, and they had to be able to work together. Pidgin evolved as an ad hoc, but surprisingly effective way to communicate, and much of it survives in slang and common usage today.

Pronunciation

Consonants are pronounced the same as in English, except that the W sometimes sounds more like a V when it appears in the middle of a word. Vowels are pronounced as follows:

a = long as in father
e = short as in den, or long as the ay in say
i = long as the ee in sea
o = round as in no
u = round as the ou in you

When vowels are joined (as they often are), pronounce each, with slightly more emphasis on the first one. This varies with local usage.

Commonly Used Vocabulary and Place Names

'a'a = rough lava (of Hawai'ian origin, now used worldwide)
'ahi = tuna, especially yellowfin (albacore) tuna
ahupua'a = land division in pie shape from mountain to sea
ali'i = chief
aloha = hello, goodbye, expressing affection
haole = foreigner (now usually meaning a white person)
heiau = temple, religious platform
hula = native Hawai'ian dance
humuhumunukunukuapua'a = trigger fish that is Hawai'ian state fish
imu = pit for steaming food over hot stones
kahuna = powerful priest
kai = sea
kama'aina = long-time resident of the islands
kane = male
kapu = taboo
ko'ala = barbequed
kokua = help
kona = leeward, or away from the direction of the wind
kukui = candlenut (state tree)
lei = garland of flowers, shells, etc. given as a symbol of affection
lu'au = Hawai'ian traditional feast, including roast pork and poi
mahalo = thanks; admiration, praise, respect
mahimahi = dolphinfish (not a dolphin)
makai = on the seaside, towards the sea, or in that direction
malihini = recent arrival to the islands, tourist, stranger
mana = power coming from the spirit world
mano = shark
mauka = upland, towards the mountains
mauna = mountain, peak
menehune = little people of legend, here before the Polynesians
moana = ocean
nene = Hawai'ian state bird
niu = coconut
ohana = extended family
ono = the best, delicious, savory; to relish or crave
pahoehoe = lava that has a smooth texture (used worldwide)
paka lolo = marijuana
pali = cliff
pupu = appetizer, snack
taro (Polynesian word) = starchy rootplant used to make poi
wahine = female
wai = fresh water
wana = sea urchin

Kahului Airport

Most flights arrive via Kahului Airport. Nearby rental cars can be reached by shuttle. The airport area is well-signed, with easy-to-find freeways heading in all directions. Large, busy gas stations are located just to the west. Plenty of shopping is available if you want to pick up supplies on your way to a condo. You'll see Costco on the left as you leave the airport area going west. The stream of arriving tourists is quite impressive, but the airport's efficiency makes it easy to get right to the beaches when arriving midday.

Kapalua West Maui Airport is much closer to the Kapalua-Ka'anapali area, avoiding the traffic across the island. However, few flights use this smaller airport.

It's possible to fly to Lana'i by way of Kahului, but it's usually easier and often faster or more convenient to fly by way of Honolulu or take the ferry from Lahaina to Lana'i.

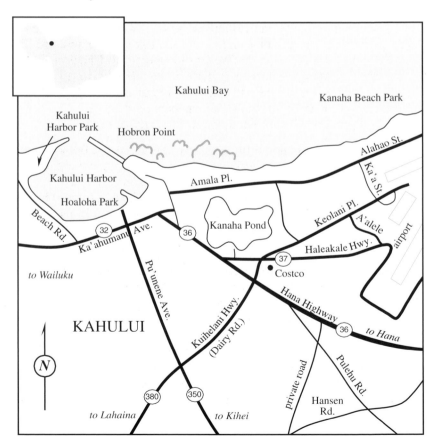

Snorkeling the Internet

We figure some of you are really wired. Brought your laptop along to poolside just for fun? Just got one of those new SportsLaptops with the rubberized keyboard? Maybe you don't even have to get out of the water to log on the net, who knows?

We like speed, too, but book writing and publishing is still a slow business. You wouldn't believe how many long, hard hours we spend slaving away, snorkeling and researching, researching and snorkeling some more, in order to produce the little volume you're holding. Maybe a hundred hours of research gets distilled into one little page of maps and text. It makes me sweat just to think about it.

Oh, yeah, *some tough job*, I hear someone saying. We get no sympathy. But we have learned to live with that, and snorkel on. To enable the wired to get the latest corrections and additions between revisions, we've created **www.snorkelguides.com** We post links to Hawai'ian resources there, as well as updates to phone numbers, excursions, and many other goodies. There are a lot of good resources on the Web, more every day. Check out our progress on other snorkeling guidebooks. Or you can find out just how to order copies to send to all your friends. A great Christmas or birthday gift, a lot better than another pair of socks for good old Dad! Encourage healthy, active snorkeling!

We'd love to hear what you like or don't like about our books, and reports about your experiences snorkeling. If you've found a great snorkeling site anywhere in the world, let us know via e-mail if you can and we'll share some of our favorites, too. The Web is changing hourly, so the best way to get current links is to go to our Web page, and just click on them!

Warning: The Web is getting more commercial. It's a libertarian's dream, anarchic, free and open, unfettered and sometimes chaotic. The downside to this unregulated utopia: you can't tell whether someone has a hidden agenda, knows what they're talking about, or is just plain lying. Watch out! Remember to maintain a healthy skepticism as you surf the web. Many of the elaborate sites are commercial, so what seems to be an objective review might have been bought and paid for. Someone selling excursions may only list those that give them a big cut. Be streetwise as you enjoy the web, and you'll be OK.

Often Heard Myths

- **"You'll probably never see a shark."**

  If you snorkel often, you probably will see one occasionally, a reef shark, not a Great White or Tiger Shark. Most sharks aren't interested in you for dinner. If you look at actual statistics, your time is better spent worrying about lightning.

- **"Barracudas are harmless to humans."**

  Perhaps some are quite innocuous, but others have bitten off fingers or hands. The Great Barracuda has been involved in the majority of cases we've read. I wouldn't worry about one that has been hanging out in front of a hotel for years, but I wouldn't crowd them either. I'd be even more cautious about eating one for dinner, because they are a definite, major cause of ciguatera "fish poisoning". They are one of the best tasting fish, though, in our experience. Feeling lucky?

- **"Jewelry attracts barracuda bites."**

  I first heard this rumor from a 12-year-old, and it was later reinforced by numerous books. The idea is that the flash will fool a barracuda into attacking. However, we've never heard of a definite case of a woman losing an ear lobe this way, even though I see people swimming and diving with earrings all the time. The same goes for wedding bands. I keep mine on.

- **"The water in Hawai'i is too cold for comfort."**
  "The water is Hawai'i is as warm as bath water."

  It can be pretty cool, especially late winter, especially if you go in naked; but there is an alternative. Just wear a thin wetsuit and it will feel a lot like the Caribbean in summer. Or you can wait till late summer and give the water a chance to warm up. Don't expect warm water in March.

- **"It rains all the time on the Maui."**
  "Maui is too hot and sunny."
  "It's always windy in Maui."

  On Maui you can have the climate of your choice. Don't believe everything you read in advertising literature (like hotel brochures) regarding perfect weather. It does vary, there are seasons, and location matters. It just depends on your personal preferences. You may hit a patch of rain, but on the west side, it seldom lasts for long. The typical weather report for Wailea is: Tonight–fair; Tomorrow, mostly sunny; for the weekend, sunny except for some upslope clouds in the afternoon. The drama of weather is part of the charm of the tropics – enjoy it as it is, rather than expecting it to be exactly as you want.

- **"Octopuses only come out at night."**

  Some types are nocturnal, some not. We've seen lots in Hawai'i quite active during the day. The hard part is spotting them! Pay your dues, look sharp, and you'll see one eventually.

- **"Maui is too crowded and commercial."**

  While there is certainly no problem buying a T-shirt in Lahaina or finding sun-worshippers in Ka'anapali, there are plenty of spectacular sites to snorkel that are completely uncrowded. As long as you have a car, it's easy to drive to delightful and secluded locations – usually within half an hour from your hotel or condo. Hiking on Maui can take you completely away from civilization as you know it, but a good map (such as ours) can lead you to some lovely snorkeling sites as well as romantic vistas to enjoy the sunset and the view of neighboring islands.

  And for really getting away from it all, try a trip to Lana'i. Pay Trilogy or Navatek to take you there with all the trimmings or enjoy a less expensive, more independent and longer day by taking the Expeditions Ferry from Lahaina.

- **"The food is too expensive."**

  Restaurant food is not inexpensive, but it also costs no more than in most major urban areas. In a grocery store, it does cost a fair amount more, especially fresh produce that must be flown in. But there are solutions. Rent a condo, pick up a trunk-load of staples at Costco as you leave the airport, and check out the great variety of foods at the local grocery Hawai'ian specialties. Try the hearty Hawai'ian "plate lunch", which is inexpensive and doesn't leave room for a full dinner. Be sure to check out the Kona coffee, local fresh fruits, Maui onions, and ever-popular bakeries and ice cream vendors. There's no reason to go hungry on Maui.

Index

oval butterflyfish

About the Authors

Judy and Mel Malinowski love to snorkel.

They have sought out great snorkeling and cultural experiences since the 70's, traveling to 60-some countries from Anguilla to Zanzibar in the process. Hawai'i keeps drawing them back, and eventually they may become kama'aina.

Although they are certified Scuba divers, the lightness and freedom of snorkeling keeps it their favorite recreation.

Mel, Judy and their three children have hosted students and cultural exchange visitors from Bosnia, Brazil, China, Germany, Nepal, New Zealand, Serbia, and Turkey in their home, and helped hundreds of other families enrich their lives through cultural exchange.

Working with exchange students and traveling as much as their businesses allow has encouraged their interest in the study of languages, from Spanish to Chinese.

Graduates of Stanford University, they live in Santa Cruz, California.